C—

THANKS SO MUCH
FOR THE REASSURANCE
THAT I FELL SHORT O
FULLY SACRELIGIOUS
YOU'RE THE TOPS,

BARE-KNUCKLED LIT

Caroline,
your arguments
are all
worth fighting
for.

BARE-KNUCKLED LIT

THE BEST OF WRITE CLUB

EDITED BY

LINDSAY MUSCATO
AND IAN BELKNAP

FOREWORD BY SAMANTHA IRBY

HOPE AND NONTHINGS
CHICAGO

Bare-Knuckled Lit: The Best of WRITE CLUB
Edited by Lindsay Muscato and Ian Belknap
ISBN 978-0-9815643-8-8
First Edition, December 2014

Printed in the United States of America.
Book design by Jason Harvey.

Distributed by Publishers Group West.

Hope and Nonthings books are available in bulk at discount prices. For more information visit hopeandnonthings.com

For Hallie, Finn, and Sadie
I remain your willing hostage.
I.B.

For P.M., and for WRITE CLUB audience members everywhere
You are mighty.
L.M.

CONTENTS

FOREWORD: Samantha Irby

The first time I competed at WRITE CLUB I totally fucking lost. Ten minutes before the show was scheduled to begin I stood wedged uncomfortably into this tiny corner of the bar bundled in a scarf with a whiskey in one hand and an inky black Sharpie in the other, reading and re-reading the piece that had run six minutes and forty-seven seconds the last time I timed it during my lunch break earlier that day. I was looking for words I could make shorter and sentences I could make punchier, because I had stood nursing my beer in the back of the Hideout a few times before feeling that sick oily feeling that climbs up the back of your throat when someone else's joke falls like a rock from the stage onto a room full of upturned faces and I was not going to let that shit happen to me. And I had also been there when a man's heartfelt, passionate defense was brutally cut short by a room full of drunks gleefully screaming, "ENHHHHH!" (or however you spell that obnoxious sound people make when imitating a buzzer, salivating for the theoretical hook to yank that ill-prepared loser off the fucking stage) as the clock ticked backward to zero, preventing him from putting the coda on the end of his piece. AND YOU HAVE TO HAVE THE FUCKING CODA. It's the juiciest goddamned part. He looked crestfallen. I felt his pain. And, if I was offered the chance, refused to ever be him.

The first time I went to WRITE CLUB I couldn't fucking believe it. I paid my ten charity dollars and got my hand stamp and my beer and edged my way into the back of the room. The Hideout was filled to capacity and electric with nerd energy. A couple people nervously shuffled wrinkled sheets of paper and murmured to themselves as they read, suiting up; others hugged and clinked glasses and compared 401k investments. I had to elbow some skinny, bearded librarian five or six times in the kidney to get him to shove over so I could properly see the goddamned stage. The lights dimmed and the music started (which, at the time, I'm pretty sure was some song by Swizz Beatz that elicited an "UGH, WHITE PEOPLE" groan and eyeroll from me even though it was kind of a jam) and the crowd started, like, for real hollering and then Ian appeared onstage in his hip dad clothes and fashionably tousled hair, screaming into the microphone from the pit of his belly. THAT SHIT WAS MOTHERFUCKING EXHILARATING.

I had been to readings before. Sedate affairs during which everyone uses his inside voice and furrows an earnest brow and isn't drunk. Adults settling in for story hour before naptime and a snack, tucked tightly into folding chairs in an unused corner of the local independent bookstore, lulled to dreamland by hushed tones recounting lame first kisses at summer camps years past or that one excruciatingly unremarkable piece of advice grandma imparted from her deathbed. You go to these things and everyone is sitting there in their cardigans, hands clasped in their laps until the appropriate times for polite applause, all of the life sucked out of the room as some drone rattles on for fifteen real minutes about the least-compelling thing you've ever goddamn heard. YES I HAVE BEEN TO THESE BORING-ASS READINGS.

But WRITE CLUB isn't just a bunch of smug assholes reading things. It isn't taciturn observation and dull appreciation. It isn't your fifth-grade book report recited in a hesitant stutter at the chalkboard in front of your bored, churlish classmates. This is brain-to-brain combat between adversaries at the top of their games, fought with words forged of brass and wrapped around knuckles made of wit, waging an intense duel of opposing ideas. WRITE CLUB is the brightest, the smartest, and the most capable. I have seen the show dozens of times and never once have I not stood at the back of that crowded room with my jaw slack, stunned by some genius turn of phrase or awed by the courage of some heartbreaking performance. And that is the brilliant thing about live lit, these readings that aren't really readings but aren't really acting either: the power that one voice can have to move you from laughter to tears and all the way back again.

BARE-KNUCKLED LIT

Anyway, I know that people laughed. I heard those fucking jerks, every single snort and guffaw, as I expertly laid out my case for UNDEAD versus DEAD. And I finished with plenty of time, even though I stumbled over a couple words because I got nervous and couldn't decipher all of my hastily scribbled notes. In the future I would go on to win, like, five of those cheap fucking trophies* Ian gives to the winners but on that day I stood vanquished, my cheeks burning hot and pink under the lights onstage as I wondered how I could *possibly* have made a piece about banging an underage *Twilight* werewolf even more hilarious than it already had been. It's the ones you lose that sting the most.

The essays in this book are really good. They are the work of some of the finest writers in Chicago, Atlanta, and San Francisco, and I am honored to be included among them. Especially since the piece I submitted won. I AM STILL NOT OVER THAT LOSS, GUYS. Prepare to have your skull peeled back while we punch you in the fucking brain.

* In WRITE CLUB parlance, The Loving Cup of Deathless Fucking Glory —eds.

INTRODUCTION

As with many sound ideas, WRITE CLUB was born of frustration, from a too-long series of bloody face prints on the brick wall of circumstance. Pro tip for you budding artists: AGONY IS THE PRICE OF ADMISSION!!!!! Additional pro tip: be judicious with exclamation points and with using all caps.

WRITE CLUB Origin Myth:

In late 2009, when the notion for this thing first seized me, I was at a pretty low goddamn ebb, I can tell you. In the long, grisly wake of the Great and Engulfing Economic Fireball of 2008, things were feeling bleak and impossible in my day job – because I was a fundraiser for a small arts non-profit, a difficult line of work under the best of circumstances, and when the accumulated wealth of a generation is set aflame, it becomes an endeavor of such monumental futility, it made going to work about as fun as lying in a puddle of cloudy garbage water all day to be beaten with wrenches.

I was also feeling totally thwarted as an artist. I was a former actor and comedian, had done a full-length solo show and a few other things, but couldn't find the cubbyhole where my stuff belonged. I'd soured on acting long before – pro tip the third: if, when auditioning for a "bite-and-smile" commercial for a regional restaurant chain, your blistering subtext is "I wish to poison you all," you may not book the gig. And I'd stopped doing standup comedy several years previous – in part because I could not travel due to kids, etc., but also because to perform standup, you've gotta hang out with comedians, who – as a class, are the most misanthropic snarl of neuroses and self-doubt you'll ever come across, and I don't need much of a nudge in that direction.

But the thing I did dig about standup was that I was writing my own stuff. And I did like the "plant your feet and counterpunch/thrive or dig your own grave" mode of performing required to be a comic. So whatever I took up next had to involve writing my own material, and it had to have a similarly bare-bones and embattled aesthetic. From standup, I stole these.

I had also come to know the work of Chicago's legendary fringe theater company The Neo-Futurists, who create what they call non-illusory theater, by which they mean that if you take the stage, you do so only as yourself, and you jettison all fakery – in short, if you have the temerity to get up in front of people, you had goddamn well better not be lying to them. So I stole that, too.

The Neos' most famous show is *Too Much Light Makes the Baby Go Blind: 30 Plays in 60 Minutes* (*TML*), which demands a great deal of its artists and its audience. For the former, it entails flinging yourself into this punishing crucible where you must write original material EVERY WEEK you are in the show. You must submit this material to the scrutiny of your ensemble-mates and be ready to perform the work publicly that weekend. For the latter, attending this show does not afford you the chance to hang back with gaping mouths as passive recipients, ready to accept the contents of mama bird's gullet. At *TML*, there can be the vertiginous mouth-drying peril of being hauled onstage by one or more of the performers, but even if this fate does not befall you, there is nonetheless the requirement that every person there be fully engaged, fully present, and fully complicit in the proceedings, no matter what strange turn they may take. I stole that, as well.

I also stole the Principle of Velocity, and the Despotic and Plainly Visible Clock That Would Ratchet Up the Stakes As Time Drains Away.

Lastly, in late 2009/early 2010, there were early rumblings of what has come to be Chicago's live lit scene (a term I coined – more on that in a sec) – a group of shows that featured original writing read by the author. I went to some of these, and found some of this work tremendously exciting, but found too many shows to be slackly run, too prone to indulgence, tending too much to disregard the audience experience, and, most criminally, too goddamn long. Much has been made of the dwindling of our collective attention span – many hands have been wrung, many tongues have clucked. And, yes, I get it – it's tempting to regard this erosion as evidence of our inexorable decline, proof that we're all growing dumber, and we're now in the earliest days of a pre-*Idiocracy* America. But this is not the case. It's more that – given the constant onslaught of stuff to read/view/like/share/link to, it's little wonder that we've each grown more merciless in our assessments.

Sidebar: Why we need the term live lit: *"storytelling" is obviously restricted to* narrative *literature, so it fails to incorporate personal essay or any other form; "author reading" sounds so boring in advance, that nobody in their right mind would voluntarily go to one.*

When every human over the age of six is pestering you around the clock to check out his unfailingly boring *Tumblr* and her vacuous fucking vlog, you are herewith forgiven if you decide right now that every bit of content passed in your direction must make it through your mental guillotine. In fact, maybe if all of us got a little more brutal in such classifications, we might elevate the standards we apply to the stuff we ourselves put into the world, as well as the culture we consume. And if we collectively agreed to that, maybe we wouldn't be saddled with James Franco.

So – these are some of the inciting impulses underlying WRITE CLUB. Shuffle these together, and you get the following formula:

3 Bouts of
2 Opposing Writers, 2 Opposing Topics Assigned in Advance
7 Minutes Apiece
Audience Picks Winners
Prize Money Goes to Charities of Victors' Choosing

In practice, a WRITE CLUB show zips along – it is a fast-paced, whip-smart, sharp-tongued smarty party that's over before you know it. On the face of it, it's just a fun and moderately priced excuse to go out and get weeknight drunk. Not drunk-drunk, but weeknight drunk. Plus, being in a WRITE CLUB crowd can have a bracingly galvanizing effect akin to Orwell's Two Minutes Hate, but without any of the dehumanizing political skullduggery – you get to yell. A lot. Publicly. Feels good.

In its impact, though, a WRITE CLUB show seeks to be more than that – yes, it adopts the bellicose tone of pro wrestling; yes, it takes the form of gladiatorial blood-letting; and yes, it traffics in glorious victory or crushing defeat. That's how it LOOKS. But underlying all that is something quite different, and a damn sight more powerful.

Over time, I've come to see WRITE CLUB as a forum for the public dissection of our convictions – a place where we can lay bare what we believe about the world. Highfalutin-sounding, I recognize. But it's really true. By accepting a one-word assignment (Fire, Death, Love, etc.), writer-performers have to grapple with how their topics connect to them directly, which means each combatant needs to unearth her own beliefs about it, and then articulate those beliefs in a cogent and compelling fashion. But what elevates a WRITE CLUB essay above the bloodless kind of expository writing we all had to do in school – we've all done time on the rock pile of What I Did This Summer – is that it's personal, yes, but it's also intended to persuade. If you don't sway the audience in your favor, your brilliance will have been squandered.

Which may have you going, "But doesn't that just constitute the worst sort of pandering party?" Nope, mostly not. Because by deputizing the crowd as Arbiters of Victory, by creating a culture where everybody aims for the top rung of the Ladder of Intelligence and Craft, and by having a Real World Purpose (i.e., money to charity) underlying the whole enterprise, we mostly sidestep the real and present danger of aiming only at Flop Sweat Avoidance, which is really only a good barometer for success if you're a middling improv troupe or an *American Idol*-style balladeer.

In addition to having made the artistic outlet that I needed personally, I have also created a show that I always wish to be in the audience for – a month doesn't go by that I'm not dazzled by some turn of phrase or novel idea, riveted by some display of courage or candor – and I'm pleased as I can be that other people, many of them, in a growing number of places, have responded with comparable enthusiasm. This is greatly heartening to me, since too much of our culture is... how can I put this delicately? A Lumbering Wagon Train of Undeserving Swine.

I hope you'll get a charge out of the essays in this book. And that you'll make your way to a WRITE CLUB near you, be it in live show or podcast form, and that you'll lace up your boots and march with us in this ongoing campaign, this incremental insurrection, this Great and Glorious Enterprise.

Many thanks.

Ian Belknap
Founder and Overlord of WRITE CLUB

NATIVE

vs

FOREIGN

NATIVE: Chloe Johnston

Imagine, if you will, that you are a smallmouth bass.

First off, you are adorable.

Those golden iridescent scales cascading down your back... That Betty Boop mouth. Sensual. Small. You are, and I quote a very reputable fishing site, a "plucky game fish that gives good fight on the line."

Well, well, well...

Native is what is here and what belongs here. It is the indigenous and the natural and the group with deepest roots. BUT — We can't deny that in this globalized, post-colonial age, we are, and should be, a little suspicious of the term. The word NATIVE has been used to delegitimize the colonized ("the natives are restless" — hint: they mean DARK people!) The word NATIVE has been adopted by conservative cranks to describe all those guys that they CLAIM were disenfranchised by our most recent election results (hint: they mean WHITE people!)

So I want to take NATIVE out of the realm of politics altogether, and wash it clean of its historical muck in the fresh, sweet waters of our closest body of water. Lake Michigan.

Back to you, a smallmouth bass, shimmering through the chilly damp atmosphere, maybe blowing a kiss to a drum fish, maybe winking at a perch (or not, cause you know, no eyelids). It's a good life. Swimming peacefully through the green-brown haze of the Greatest of Great Lakes. The world is not your oyster but your delicious local crayfish...

When all of a sudden, it's coming at you — the gaping maw, a huge hole in the middle of the lake, framed by teeth. You are staring into the abyss. Then your eyes meet the eyes of this creature. (I mean this metaphorically, because not only do you not have eyelids, your eyes are actually on the side of your head.) You are looking down the throat of your own destruction.

You may have heard of the terrifying ASIAN CARP. The possible invasion of this species of hulking meaty fish, gnashing at the water around them, their bottomless hunger, their rapacious need to eat everything in sight sends environmentalists into a frothy panic. They don't belong here, the Asian Carp. Their presence destroys the delicate balance. They are *the foreign*, and they will destroy the native.

And you, the innocent little fish, just trying to swim around. Is it your fault that globalization, that the rapid speed at which every beast, fish or fowl can now travel to parts of the globe where they were never meant to be, means that your very ability to gurgle and spawn should be threatened by prehistoric monsters from Asia?

It is not.

It is our fault. The humans. We enjoy our first-world access to cheap electronics that sending boats around the world allows. The destructive foreign influence has merely hitched a ride on our greed. But still, the native will pay.

Now I am fully aware of the racial undertones to this story. Lest you fear that I espouse any sort of xenophobic, nativist philosophy, let me assure you that I am big fan of the human Asian-American community, having gone so far as to MARRY an Asian-American. For you see, my husband was raised by foreigners.

And let me tell you, no one loves all things deeply, disgustingly American like a man who was a little boy with two heavily accented parents. He's at home right now figuring out how to deep fry a turkey, for god's sake.

I'm glad his parents were both brave enough to become foreigners in a strange land. I love foreigners. We live in a city which seems by definition a celebration of the foreign. Cities are the places where foreigners arrive, where they buy cheap property and open restaurants. Where they get their footing in a new world, and I am thankful for that — for both ethical and culinary reasons. But that is merely the built environment. Nature, the thing that is native by definition, peeks through the cracks in the pavement, the spaces between parking lots. There are places you can stand, on the shores of Lake Michigan, within the city limits, where you can watch the native grasses swaying, and listen to the birds who have sung the same songs since long before you came here.

Everything I know about the native smallmouth bass I learned from the aforementioned turkey frier, my own little Asian Carp. He has dragged me out to the lakefront at ungodly hours of the morning to go fishing. Here you see Polish grandfathers, sipping their Ice Mountain beer as the sun comes up. Vietnamese men who have arrived on bicycles, balancing heavy buckets as they pedal. Men from places in Africa I can't identify, whispering rapid French to one another. They each love the lake. They trade tips and disagree about which of the native species is the tastiest. And if you walk past them on an early morn, you'll see them periodically pull a fish from the lake, frown at it, and throw it behind them to be fed to the seagulls. Foreign, invasive species.

These foreigners share one thing: a love of the native.

FOREIGN: Mary Fons

You can't choose your birthplace, your native land. But you can choose the fuck out of where you wanna go.

You're "from" Modesto. You *live* in Rome.

You're "from" a family that traffics in burnt ham and thinly veiled hate. You *practice* patience and serve fennel most delicious.

You didn't learn that at home! Did you! No, you did not. A foreign agent was introduced at some point. A stranger. A new strand. A foreign idea that went viral in your native, previously static brain. Often this sort of thing comes from a book, and we all know a book opens like a door. *Foreign* comes from the Latin *foras,* which means "door." What can possibly be accomplished if you don't open the door? A closed room? What air comes in, what breath? None can come. Perhaps more depressing: none can leave.

You stay in one place, you start collecting dust and Precious Moments figurines.

Just ask my estranged, senile grandmother presently mellowing in her Texas nursing home. I'm glad she's in her *native* city of Houston. That's surely a comfort to her, being there among the familiar faded church bulletins pinned to familiar, beige walls.

Of course, if she had gone to Dubai, instead of marrying the first man who gave her a moment's notice back home, she might not be gumming bland, pureed carrots right now. Oh, it might be carrots. She's ninety: it's gonna be carrots. But it might be *curried* carrots, and if it were, if she had eaten more curry over the course of her life, it might've aided her digestion, which curry is believed to do, and this would have ultimately benefited her DNA, which would've been passed on to my dad, who likely would've married a different woman than my mother if he had gone to Cordoba instead of *also* staying in Houston. And sure, I'd be a different Mary, maybe with more almond-shaped eyes, tooling around muddy side roads in a beat-up Gremlin looking for work, but I'd probably be singing to a quality, new-*ish* American pop song, and I would *not* likely have spent four days in the hospital last week, as I did, due to complications from a disease I think I got from my grandmother. Undoubtedly I'd have a different set of problems (we are all unhappy in our own ways) but to be rid of the pathogen that developed, naturally, hereditarily, — natively if you will — in my abdomen, well, I'd roll those dice in a banana-leaf minute.

No, you can't choose who your natives are or where you're "from." But you choose the foreign places you *go*, and if you are a serious person, aware that you are here for one shot and one shot only, with no "do-over," no eternal party to look forward to if you're "nice"; if you are soaked in the reality of this lovely and shatteringly painful moment that you have chanced upon — entirely owing to a *foreign object* entering your mom's, you know, ehhh, word to your mom — if you are *alive*, good people, you *want to go*, not just "go on." You want to go to Perth, or Venus, or dinner at the new place and you want to go now, and go away, and go farther, and go big and keep going. Keep going. I know, it's fuckin' hard.

It's so hard and then, what do we do when we can't take it anymore? We get out! We throw him or her or *it out*. We welcome the door, the *foras*, hitting us in the ass, we wait for it, the door hitting us, it's pragmatic, it gives us the extra push. We escape to a foreign place, click through to a plane ticket purchase. We pack a change of panties, a phrasebook, or nothing, or a noose, or a set of shiny new razorblades and we leave (oh yes, we have all kinds of ways to go) because what is foreign — while it is uncertain, indeed, and risky, of course, and frightening, yes — what is foreign is *better than what we know*. We do know that.

The foreign is better than the leftovers in the fridge that never get fresher; better than the preset radio station that insists on being the same gesture away from the steering wheel, day in, day out; it's better than the same old cereal flakes, the same worn satchel, the same old you, regardless of profile pic. What's unknown is certain to be better than the objects in our native habitat: the chair, the chair, *the fucking chair.* Familiarity breeds contempt, *contempt, I hate you I hate you you chair you lout you bore you constant cracked-milk-pitcher-with-the-flower-motif-on-the-side you moth-eaten-closet-of-dead-eyed-dresses staring at me again, you standard, typical, native beasts! I'm gone! I'm gone!* I'm leaving and I am not coming back with the same eyes. It would be impossible once I step out and meet the foreign skies and the rearranged figurines on the streets. I cannot come back the same, which is to say that "I" will never come back. Which is the goal.

A new version of ourselves, that is what we want, what we eternally want. It's what we want when we buy. It is what we want when we drink. When we answer the ad for used furniture or new love, however used up it may reveal itself to be. Our desire to be foreign to our very selves is in every haircut, every diet change, every cataloged course we select, every new job we take, every current endeavor for business or pleasure, every date, every first kiss at any bar in Chicago tonight, any night, every night of the same old seven-day week. We want what we don't have. It is the drive of our species. From the C-average sorority pledge to the lettered scientist — make no mistake, the latter is in the lab as we speak, introducing a foreign agent into the dish.

"Tomorrow is a brand new day!" they exclaim, cheerily.

Why such confidence?

Because tomorrow is foreign. *You just don't know.* What hurt on Monday, well, it just might not be so bad on Tuesday, you don't know! So get up, sunshine! Carpe tomorrow, motherfucker! Tomorrow is different, foreign to us and fresh! Forget the congenital, native today and its attendant malaise. Who needs it? *Nobody.* Nobody needs it. I am proud to meet every dawn a foreigner.

It's tomorrow that we live for. The foreign nature of it, the strange that gets us out of our creaking, musty, painfully native beds.

Cast your totally uncountable vote for the winner:

☐ NATIVE: Chloe Johnston

☐ FOREIGN: Mary Fons

ANGELS

VS

DEMONS

ANGELS: Nicholas Tecosky

I. JERRY

Pyro Jerry died a couple of months back.

He'd disappeared years ago, without any trace, and when I'd asked around work whether anyone had heard from him, they shrugged, disinterested. Nobody even feigned curiosity about his fate. So I decided to seek him out. After all, if *I* disappeared, I would want someone to come looking for me. It took ten days of calling around and scouring the Internet, but I finally found out that he was alive and alone and sick and bored. He needed a friend. So having located him, I promptly forgot that he existed.

I am unsurprised to meet him one night at Dottie's, sitting quietly at a table listening to a couple of drunk assholes try and one-up each other retelling "The Aristocrats" poorly. He listens raptly until he sees me. He smiles genially but does not get up. I sit down and join him. He pours from a bottle into my glass.

"Hi," I say.

"Hey," he says.

"You're dead," I say.

He nods.

"Two months now," he says, in that quiet way he always had of saying things. For a man so big to have a voice so meek was always jarring.

"How was it? Dying?"

"Lonely."

I shift uncomfortably on the stool.

"Hey. I'm sorry about... not being around. Or calling. Or not answering any of your Facebook posts. Ever."

Pyro Jerry raises his glass to me.

"God save you from friends like yourself, Tecosky."

It seems harsh, but after thinking about it, I can see he has a point.

2. DOTTIE

I dream of the bar regularly.

It's only found in locations that should harbor no bar. In the middle of the beach at Edisto Island, once. Once it was the living room of my childhood living home. Wherever my dream places it, there it is. Though there is no sign, I inherently know that it is called Dottie's, though I could not for the life of me tell you why. I only knew one Dottie, ever, a girl in my playwriting course sophomore year, and if we ever spoke more than a handful of words, I'd forgotten them. She was a pretty girl, nice, but a terrible writer and an uninquisitive student. That's all I remember of her. But there it is. Dottie's. In my backyard or on top of Stone Mountain or on the moon. Dirty place. Cracked patio furniture. Dog-eared posters taped haphazardly to the walls. They only serve one type of liquor, and it's bitter like aspirin, but it goes down smooth.

The bar is populated by dead friends. They seem comfortable enough there, if bored. They usually nod politely when I enter and go back to their arguments about who that actress in *Norma Jean and Marilyn* was. It was Mira Sorvino, I say, but they ignore me.

The dead always seem to have more pressing matters to attend to than I.

3. FATHER

Christmas 1990. The first after the divorce. A desperate struggle to pretend to not be unhappy. Manic smiles plastered on each face. Dad has twisted himself into knots trying to make his poor apartment festive, and my siblings and I appreciate it, though still I feel an ache deep in my gut that cannot be put into words by an 11-year-old.

During dinner, I look up at the television screen, where *The Incredible Mr. Limpet* plays on mute. I can't follow the storyline entirely, but Don Knotts is a cartoon fish who fights Nazis. A hero for our time.

Somehow, watching *this*, I sense the beginnings of the man I am to become.

4. MICHAEL

At Dottie's, The Archangel Michael is always behind the bar. He seems to have family problems of his own.

He opines, throwing back a bitter shot: "I don't know what the deal is. So he died painfully. So do most of you assholes. Everybody talks about the water into wine thing. What they never tell you is that he makes shitty wine. One time he came *this close* to making an Ernest and Julio Gallo Zinfandel. Close. Most of the time, it's just Manischewitz."

He clutches his head in his hands. I know what he's about to say.

"I shouldn't be here. You shouldn't be here. This shouldn't be here. What are we doing here, what are we always doing here? And why is it always Christmastime here? It is always Christmas, 1990. *The Incredible Mr. Limpet* is always playing on the TV on mute.

"Don Knotts has lost all meaning here. He's just a man who is a fish who is a naval officer. THIS MOVIE NEVER MAKES SENSE TO ME WHY IS A FISH A NAVAL OFFICER?"

On the television, Don Knotts lets out a silent scream. Being a naval officer is not all that he had expected, apparently. But then, War is Hell.

Even for a fish.

5. NICHOLAS

The Archangel is right: Why always a bar?

And if a bar, why one as shitty and run down as Dottie's?

In my waking hours, I turn this question over and over in my head. It never makes sense until I'm halfway through my third drink of the night, a flicker of warm light. In that glass: clarity.

Each dead patron, I see, is an old regret, a secret shame brought to life to walk and play darts and sing old dirges. When they look at me, I can see that I have been a bad friend, a bad son, a lazy and listless writer, negligent in my duties.

What's more, I will never address them sober. Instead, I will trap them there, to stay, in the warm, forgiving light of drunkenness.

I am safe in this glow. I am most myself in it, so much myself that I return there in my dreams, to Dottie's, the only place where I am able to face the litany of regrets chanted forever in my head.

This method of introspection may well kill me. In a matter of years, it will become a regret of its own, fully personified, skulking about, sharply dressed in monocle and checkered coat, leering up at me from its barstool, pushing a bottle of Dottie's bitter brew across the table, inviting me to stay.

DEMONS: Jason Mallory

Years ago, I found myself in a strip club called Lucifer's Follies, where the only dancer had a tattoo that read "100% pure USDA inspected beef" on her inner thigh. Finally, the food packaging industry's greatest achievement — food that inspects itself and, finding itself acceptable, wraps and labels itself before walking itself out on the shelf.

I didn't think her tattoo was entirely official. Then again, if you're feeling like you're being treated like a piece of meat, you might as well get it notarized. Just because the government doesn't recognize your declaration of exploitation doesn't mean you shouldn't go ahead and fill out the paperwork.

She looked like an orc from *The Lord of the Rings*, but also kind of hot? Like if J. R. R. Tolkien had followed *The Silmarillion* with a series of Tijuana Bibles. She was the bootleg Bart Simpson T-shirt of fuckable orcs.

She was dancing for the only other guy in Lucifer's Follies, a hangdog man in an old-fashioned hat who looked like he belonged in a Norman Rockwell painting where people are looking surprised at a fish they caught, or at a milkshake they're drinking from with multiple straws, or at the length of a basset hound's ears.

One thing this man was not looking surprised at was her huge, rogue-USDA-inspector-approved ass hovering mere inches from his face. If this was the Lucifer from the sign, those were not the kinds of follies he was interested in.

Then again, the sign didn't mention whether or not Lucifer enjoyed the follies, only that there were follies to be had there, and that they were, in fact, Lucifer's. I think we can all agree that ownership does not guarantee enjoyment. Who among us hasn't grown downright sick of our own follies?

Many years later, I was the recipient of a fax from a stripper named Blondie at the newspaper where I worked. Blondie was and continues to be famous for crushing empty PBR cans between her enormous breasts at the Clermont Lounge, Atlanta's first and longest continually operating strip club.

She sent me the fax to thank me for putting her picture in an article on notable Atlanta citizens, not to threaten to crush all of my cans of PBR, as she might have done if I had been the CEO of Pabst. That guy should sleep with one eye open, because she's going to single handedly take down the Pabst corporation, one can at a time (or to be more specific, two cans at a time). At least until he innovates by developing a line of PBR cans that grow their own breasts to crush the cans of his competitors with, continuing the tradition of the greatest innovations in an industry being the ideas of underappreciated third parties implemented on a global scale.

Although it shouldn't be that hard for him to sleep with one eye open, because not being able to close one eyelid is a side effect of drinking too much PBR.

The next time I was at the Clermont, I grabbed her arm and yelled, "Hey, Blondie! I work at the newspaper!" like Jimmy Olsen on his first day as a cub reporter. "I got your 'Thank You' fax! I put you in the paper!"

No reaction whatsoever. It was like I wasn't even talking to her. I may as well have been the pole-dancing orc stripper trying to get Lucifer to pay attention to my hobbit hole.

That confusingly sexy orc would have been right at home dancing at The Clermont Lounge. Or sitting on J. R. R. Tolkien's lap. His lap in the past, when he was still alive, not his modern lap, which is no doubt made of bones. Then again, if there were such a thing as lap dances for skeletons, the Clermont Lounge would be the place to see it.

If only we could open a portal in time and create a link to the past on the laps of people from bygone eras so strippers from the future could sit on them. We could send some Clermont Lounge strippers back to the World's Columbian Exposition in 1893 Chicago, setting off a chain of events in which Pabst never won its famous blue ribbon, and in which an alternate present day is created where Blondie uses her breasts to crush copies of *The Hobbit* at The Clermont Used Book Store, which is what it has become in a world without PBR.

I'm sure if time-traveling lap dances were a viable form of temptation, Lucifer would have already incorporated it into his follies. Then again, every naked lady he's not throwing through time and space at a potential sinner's lap is another soul he won't be faxing to his demon friends. That's what Lucifer wants all those souls for, right? For faxing? The souls of the damned are what make that horrible beeping noise every time someone accidentally dials the fax line for Hell instead of the phone line.

Even though the CEO of Pabst might have appreciated being thanked for thanking me in a thank-you fax, and would have probably sent me another thank-you fax just to make sure I knew how thankful he felt, as soon as he got done forcing his eyelid closed in the executive bathroom he shares with the Milwaukee's Best CEO, where they stand at the sink and inadvertently wink at one another, I have to side with Blondie on this one.

After my attempts to get her attention went ignored, someone handed her an empty PBR can. She pushed her breasts around it like a pair of basset hound's ears around the head of a surprised man in an old-fashioned hat. When the can crumpled under her might, the crowd cheered. Blondie was not there to talk about newspapers and faxes. She was there to crush beer cans with her prodigious knockers.

Huge tits are surprisingly common in this world. Everyone wants to treat you like a piece of meat. There are many follies to be had in this world, but they all belong to Lucifer. In the end, the choices we make about what we do with our amazing tits are what belongs to us.

Some of us choose to painstakingly demolish the entire inventory of a beloved national brewery. Some of us get a refreshingly honest tattoo.

The devil may never officially recognize our declarations of exploitation — but that doesn't mean we shouldn't go ahead and fill out the paperwork.

Cast your totally uncountable vote for the winner:

☐ ANGELS: Nicholas Tecosky

☐ DEMONS: Jason Mallory

ROOTS

vs

BRANCHES

ROOTS: Justin Goldman

When I say roots, what do you see? Maybe some of you are hip-hop heads, and you see rappers playing instruments. You see Questlove's afro, pick sticking out of it. I can get behind that, those are some roots. But then those dudes branched out, and where'd they end up? Backing up Jimmy Fallon. And you tell me — would you rather have the roots Roots, the *Never Do What They Do* Roots, or branched-out bantering with that smirky motherfucker Jimmy Fallon Roots?

Or maybe you're like me, and you saw the TV series *Roots* when you were a kid. Alex Haley, the author, that guy *is Roots*. But when you think about Alex Haley's *Roots*, you also gotta think about LeVar Burton. You can't help it — dude was Kunta Kinte. That was LeVar's big break, and then he branched out, did *Reading Rainbow*. Now, don't get me wrong; I got all the love in the world for *Reading Rainbow*. Hell, I wouldn't be standing up here tonight if *Reading Rainbow* hadn't told five-year-old Justin that I could fly twice as high as that butterfly in the sky. But after *Reading Rainbow*, LeVar kept branching out, and he ended up on *Star Trek*, with that weird gold visor thing on his face, and now every time you see LeVar Burton, you see blind *Star Trek* LeVar Burton, even when you're watching *Roots*.

But let's back up, go more basic than that. You think of roots, you think of trees. And when you think of a tree's roots, you probably think that they keep a tree where it is, that a tree always stays in the same place, and that a tree's roots are what keeps it in that place. But I don't necessarily look at it that way.

I don't think roots have to keep you in one place. Anybody who knows me even a little bit can tell you that I am a restless motherfucker. When I'm in the Bay, I tell people I'm from New York. When I'm in NYC, I claim SF. Shit, I've been on this stage for what, two minutes? — and I'm already working on my exit strategy. But that doesn't mean I don't have roots. My roots run deep, but I take them everywhere with me. Because roots aren't about staying in one place.

They're not about holding to one frame of mind. They're not about doing things the same way you've always done them. They *are* about staying true to who you are, about never forgetting what you set out to accomplish.

You know how sometimes you'll be walking through the city, and you'll catch yourself tripping on a jagged chunk of sidewalk? Most of the time, that pothole's there 'cause there's a big tree nearby with roots that are tearing the pavement apart, stronger than an earthquake, like an inexorable, silent jackhammer that will never, ever, ever stop. That's the strength my roots give me: to know that no matter what I encounter, I will never stop chasing my goals.

I once saw a tree growing right out of the top of a boulder. True story. The trunk ran smack into the top of this giant rock, and then all these roots snaked out around the boulder, homing in on the ground, wrapping around the rock like the strands of a spiderweb around a fly. What those roots were saying was, rock beats scissors, but roots beat rock. They were saying, we are stronger than stone. They were saying, you can't break me.

Seriously, look at me up here. Do I look especially strong to any of you? Nah, I'm short, scrawny, blind, bald, nerdy, Jewish — you name it. And honestly, I gotta admit there are times I have thought about giving up. On everything. You try to become a writer, and you watch editor and agent and publisher reject every fucking thing you do. You get picked apart in a workshop by a writer who's your hero, which is bad enough, and then you get some bratty fucking kid who's barely growing facial hair chiming in with his opinions. And then you find out that kid is actually getting shit published or going to an awesome school, and meanwhile you're two years out of a grad school it took five years to get into and your student loan debt is hanging over your head like a guillotine, and you're thirty years old and you can't afford your rent and you're still eating ramen for dinner every fucking night, and you're like fuck you *Reading Rainbow*, and fuck you LeVar Burton, 'cause you got me into this and I'm not any good and I never was any good and even if I was, no one's ever gonna actually read my shit, so what's the point?

And then somebody you love dies. And all you can think is that none of this means anything, that our lives are all hopeless and pointless and meaningless. And you find yourself floating on that wave of despair, reaching for something to grab onto, and what do you grab but a bottle that only drags you further out to sea. And when at last you feel like that's it, like you really can't go on, that all that's left is to find something high to jump off, the last place left to look for answers is inside yourself. And when you look there, you find your roots. Those roots are the people who came before you, the ones who gave you the strength to face the storm and never give an inch, the ones who've left this world, but will never leave you. And you take ink to your body, and the tattoo needle frees the roots inside you to burst through your skin, like the roots of city trees bursting through sidewalks. And you take ink to the page, because you're a writer, and the only way to be true to yourself, and to those you love, and to your roots, is to keep going.

BRANCHES: Casey A. Childers

January 17, 1862
SUBJECT: TRAVEL STATUS
Dearest Management,

We arrive, this night, with little occasion and few casualties among our number in what is soon to be the regional hub of our great western expansion. Tomorrow we set about the task of breaking ground.

On a positive note, the men appear eager for labor, not one among them wasting HIS handful of idle moments to Tweet our safe arrival or even to update his Facebook status before taking up the chores of making camp and tending to the horses.

They are good men, these men... which brings me to less joyful news.

The commander of our armed convoy has cited THE INNUMER-ABLE difficulties outlined within my prior correspondence AS CAUSE to alter our arrangement and demand a higher bounty for THE safe passage HE and his team so ably provided. As I am in no position to barter with company lucre, I am left to throw the problem upon my betters.

As collateral for these negotiations, the man has seen fit to hold our stores of salt-pork, whisky, hard-tack, and other rations in the guarded larders of his train until an adequate sum has been both agreed upon and produced.

A reasonable man, if brusque, he has agreed to spare to us a week's worth of rations — enough, he insists, to allow for a timely and thoughtful weighing of his demands.

The men crave bread and libations, sirs, and in so trying times as these, one wonders at how quickly such wants might erode Christian patience.

Respectfully,
James Maddersly
Director of Western Division Operations, Mid-Northern Branch
The Corporation

January 17, 1862

SUBJECT: Out of Office Auto-Reply

Our offices will be closed through January 20th in observance of George Washington's Birthday.

Should your matter require immediate attention, please redirect all communication to Berthold Mumfry, director of technical support.

The Corporation

"The Best has Yet To Come" ™

January 17, 1862

SUBJECT: See Attached

Mr. Mumphry,

Please find attached my earlier correspondence with the tenders of our firm. Note SPECIFICALLY the financial matter which demands immediate resolution.

Yours,

James Maddersly

Sent from my iPhone

January 18, 1862

SUBJECT: Re: See Attached

James,

You made it! We've all been eager for news.

Sadly, your problem falls beyond my departmental purview.

The Director of Logistics (WHICH is who I think actually handles these sorts of things) is out of the office until Tuesday.

Best wishes, though, and I hope to see you at the directors' conference in the fall. We're expecting big things from you WESTERN boys back here at central.

Yours,

bert

Sent from my Verizon Wireless BlackBerry

January 20, 1862

SUBJECT: Growing difficulty

Mr. Mumphry,

I have copied the Director of Logistics, as you've noted his importance in this matter, however my means of communication are desperately limited and the situation is spiraling with a quickness toward some DIRE finale.

Yesterday saw good labor and fair cheer among the men, despite a general sentiment of discontent among their number, but today has PROVED a defeat in every way, and I fear MY Masters in Business Administration has left me wanting in ability to resolve our gathering problems.

In the first, my attempts to negotiate a release of our stores with the convoy's COMMANDER have seen no fruit. Our operational account is all but dry and he will not relent in his claim of funds WHICH far outstrip those afforded by BOTH our petty-cash store AND my family's humble pension of "mad money." I went so far as to offer a sizable portion of my personal stock in THIS VERY expansion enterprise, but we could find no joy between us.

In the second, the wild-eyed steward of the Bricklayer's Union, a man called Flynn, took to a stump and called for general work stoppage with a RHYTHMIC sermon on the absurdity of a tree whose LEAVES strive toward the sun's warmth whilst its ROOTS wither in SALTED soil. No botanist, perhaps, but I'll admit that even I felt swayed by his words and FIND no wonder in the results among the men.

They mean to have their whisky, to be blunt, and if WE SHAN'T provide it then THEY MEAN to withhold their labor in the foremost and take up their TOOLS as weapons in the last.

Bold words, indeed, and I would take them as WORDS ALONE if not for the conviction of this young steward, this fair-haired FLYNN with his tattoos and his tattered Men at Work T-shirt.

In defense of my fears, I found today a number of the lads checked in to a new location called MUTINY, which the GPS shows to be within a mile of our camp, and the number of check-ins increases with each refresh of the page.

The commander has doubled his armed guard of the train, and I have sent my wife and daughters THIS NIGHT to take refuge in the mountains until I can be certain of their safety.

Please advise.

Humbly,

James Maddersly

The Corporation

JANUARY 20, 1862

SUBJECT: Out of Office Auto-Reply

Our offices will be closed through January 20th in observance of GEORGE WASHINGTON'S BIRTHDAY.

Best wishes.

Steven Augustine

Director of Logistics

The Corporation

"The Best has Yet To Come" ™

JANUARY 21, 1862

MEMORANDUM

ATTN: BRANCH MANAGERS;

There is in the works a grand and majestic marketing message for the multinational superpower we are POISED to become. There will be a consistent brand across the enterprise. We are due to have this in hand between late March and early April. Once IN HAND and board-approved, your offices shall receive details RE: its use.

You may BEGIN along our course, however, by implementing the following verbiage when describing our product:

THE CORPORATION:

BUSINESS IS OUR BUSINESS;

BUSINESS IS GOOD. ™

These words should replace all regional phrases implemented on existing letterhead for both intra- and extra-office communications. The Central Controller has been advised RE: stationary provisions and restocking.

Much exciting growth is in store, both FOR OUR organization and FOR OUR glorious brand. You men are among a select few, and you shall be remembered as heroes when THESE DAYS are but a single page from our grand endeavor's storied history.

Carry on,

Lyle Burdett

Director of New Media

THE CORPORATION:

BUSINESS IS OUR BUSINESS;

BUSINESS IS GOOD. ™

January 21, 1862

SUBJECT: (blank)

As you read these words, I am slain. The uprising against the commander and his men has proved an ugly failure, and THE SOIL DRINKS the blood of Flynn and his faithful.

I am to be made an example of and hanged before the remaining men of our party who are to be held along with our land-claim as collateral until the commander is REWARDED appropriately for his efforts.

I cannot thank you gentlemen enough for this opportunity, and all I can offer in return are my most sincere apologies AND my earnest embrace of our new marketing initiative.

Give word to my wife, should she survive the winter.

Yours,

James Maddersly

Former Director of Western Division Operations, Mid-Northern Branch

The Corporation

BUSINESS IS OUR BUSINESS;

BUSINESS IS GOOD. ™

Cast your totally uncountable vote for the winner:

☐ ROOTS: Justin Goldman

☐ BRANCHES: Casey A. Childers

LEAVE

vs

RETURN

LEAVE: Bobbin Wages

The action of leaving has done a lot of good in my life. It particularly has profited my vagina. I'll start with a story about the woman who used to be my soulmate gynecologist.

It's almost impossible to find a reputable gynecologist who earns your return business. Most gynos are judgmental hypocrites who treat their patients like cattle, herding their legs open to fetch a cervical sample before sending them on their way. A few years ago I finally had found my dream gynecologist and sought her service for my routine physical.

I lowered my torso to the end of the exam table and secured my feet in the stirrups. With her trademark sensitivity, Dr. Slater pointed the spotlight on my genitalia. Dr. Slater and I always made pleasant small talk, so when she inserted the speculum, I expected to discuss the new David Sedaris book or the piece of folk art hanging beside a poster describing the symptoms of various STDs.

She swabbed my cervix and asked without lifting her gaze, "Is there any chance you'd be interested in dating my son?"

My vagina tensed, nearly chopping her Q-tip in half while I processed the question.

"Yeah. Sure. I mean, how old is he?"

"Alessandro is in his 30s. He does the lighting for a bunch of music venues around the city. He has dreadlocks, so he's kind of a hippie," she chuckled.

While Dr. Slater completed the swab, I lay there wondering what kind of impression my vagina made to make her want to set me up with her son. Did she find my vagina so well-trimmed and clean that only it was fit for her son's perfect penis? Or did she assess its coloring and curvature as mediocre, posing no aesthetic threat to her son's average cock? Or worse, since she called her son a hippie, did my pubic landscaping remind her of a bedheaded granola girl?

"If it's alright with you, I'll give him the phone number from your chart," she confirmed.

I imagined how the conversation would go.

"Son, I performed a pap smear today on a young woman with a beautiful vagina. I think you'd really like it. Here's her phone number. You should give her a call."

A couple days later, Alessandro texted to invite me to a community pig roast. I looked him up on Facebook, unsurprised to find him half-naked in 99% of his photos tubing down a river or holding a locally grown squash. I asked Alessandro for the details on the pig roast, but he never responded.

The probability of visiting yet another judgmental hypocrite of a gynecologist remained too high, so I decided to schedule my next physical with Dr. Slater and risk potential awkwardness. However, when I called her office the receptionist informed me that Dr. Slater had fallen in love and moved to Seattle.

Dr. Slater's leaving town prevented me from further ruminating over what other girls she had attempted to introduce to her son based on the intricate folds of their labia, or from staring at my vagina in a handheld mirror, obsessing over what personality traits it suggested via its sophisticated Pablo Picasso-like lines and ambrosia-esque odors. Because Dr. Slater left, I slowly recovered from severe vaginal anxiety. Thank God Dr. Slater left town and never came back.

Let's rewind to a time when I didn't have to worry about going to the gynecologist. I was more than halfway through college, home for the summer – and a frustrated but guilt-ridden virgin. After running into my high school boyfriend in Walmart, I agreed to go "for a walk" with him around midnight the same night. Buckley refused to bring me inside his parents' house, so we sat in the front yard in his van making out and dry humping. I never had dry humped anything before except my stuffed moose, so it completely blew my mind.

Once Buckley realized nothing else was going to happen, he sighed and asked, "Do you mind if I masturbate?"

"No... go ahead..." I shrugged.

Buckley pulled out his penis and began violently swiping it and moaning. I never had seen a penis before, except the black-and-white drawings in my father's copy of *The Joy of Sex*, so I was shocked to discover that penii aren't pink like dogs' red rockets.

Upon Buckley's climax he screamed like a little girl: "Ah, ah, ayeeeyeyayayaaahhhh!"

He cleaned up the mess with his boxers.

"Aren't you going to return the favor?" he asked.

"No thank you," I answered, sliding on my pedal pushers and shoes. "I should leave."

Buckley lived on one of the most beautiful roads in the county, so I loved driving across it on the way to town, even though the scenic route added 20 minutes to my travel time. I always looked forward to coasting past the rundown Texaco station that still advertised gas for 79 cents a gallon, the fields dotted with cows, and the cemetery where my mother's best friend was buried.

All of a sudden on my ride home, one of my favorite landmarks, a corn silo, became a symbol for a menacing penis. My chest tightened, and I began to hyperventilate, reminded of my stagnant sexuality. I resolved to avoid taking the scenic route at least for a while, enabling me to preserve my purity for an entire two weeks.

Yeah, it's kind of sad. Despite our perverse first date, Buckley and I continued seeing each other. After a couple weeks of his unyielding coercion, I decided to get my virginity loss over with.

The cruel mauling of my hymen catapulted me into a spiral of on-again, off-again relationships and vaginal torture. I would leave men who weren't right for me but eventually return, fueled by shame and guilt over having sex. I believed God or my parents or some other authoritative figure would judge me for my number, and that because I had sex with someone, I was obligated to make the relationship work until a divine power overtook my body and orchestrated the long overdue breakups for me.

I finally cultivated my own set of values and left the toxicity of the Southern Baptist faith — it, too, became a relationship I would leave and return to, leave and return to.

Only when I shirked my low self-esteem and childhood spoon-fed dogma would I learn to demand respect and constant cunnilingus, and realize the action of leaving doesn't make me a quitter. Because I left the sources of my misery behind, my vagina died but rose again, not like Jesus but like a half-mangled carnation that perks up after being sprinkled with that plant food powder stuff.

I still haven't found a replacement gynecologist, though, so if you have a good one to recommend, please let me know.

RETURN: Bill Taft

My son is a 9th grader and plays the alto saxophone. He recently auditioned for the All State Band. A big deal. Kids in the All State Band get access to free lessons and programs and the chance to travel. My son wanted to be in that band. He practiced his scales and etudes for weeks. But the more he practiced the more nervous he became. He feared being rejected by the judges, coming out of the audition room, knowing that he had failed because he was stupid, ugly, not talented, smelly, poorly dressed, *guilty* of all the charges that bullying inner voice accused him of.

The more nervous he became, the harder it was to practice his saxophone.

I am the dad. My job is to bestow wisdom. And so I offered my son, a week before his audition, a life lesson learned from recent experience.

"You know, Son, failure is always relative," I told him as we drove home after school. "Just last week I was playing music with a friend on the Cabbagetown side of the Krog St. Tunnel. 9:00 at night. I played trumpet, my friend Brian played saxophone.

"We played in a little park across the street from a bar and I was nervous and afraid that the small audience of passers by would hear my mistakes and laugh at me. You see, I'm not very good at reading music and all the songs we were playing that night came from sheet music. Key signatures confound me. Sixteenth notes look like malignant blackheads adorned with sinister pirate flags. I like improvising. But Brian and I weren't there to improvise. We were there to play hit songs from the year in which tunnel construction began, 1912. Songs like 'My Melancholy Baby' and 'The Memphis Blues.' We play the songs and its like we are back in time. Maybe a century ago, while they were working on the tunnel, one of the workers may have whistled one of the tunes.

"Well that night was a bad night for me. I kept misreading notes and a voice in my head kept saying, 'You suck.' But I didn't give up and the crowd grew. A few people applauded after each song and my confidence increased. But then I heard a voice outside my head, a high-pitched, strangely slurred, and snarky voice:

Boring.

Let's sing along, not really.

My grandmother would love you guys.

"Be cool, I thought. Maybe the heckler will go away. But he didn't. And his comments grew stranger.

We should go back into the bar and rape everyone.

"Why is he saying this stuff? I wondered. Or is it a she? I can't see who is making sarcastic comments because I have to focus on the sheet music. The timber of the voice is androgynous. Do you know what androgynous means, Son?"

"Like a guy and a girl mixed up?"

"Yeah. that's about right. So I suffered through the heckling. After each wise crack I'd look up a tiny bit from the sheet music on my stand. I could see the crowd's feet and ankles. Was the voice coming from the guy in the Adidas shell-toe sneakers or the girl in the high heels? The more I studied the feet, the more I failed to read the sheet music. A vicious cycle.

"At the end of 'My Melancholy Baby,' I connect the heckler to a body.

"It's a tall guy dressed as a woman, looking very nice in a magenta sweater set. And the withering barrage of sarcasm continues. I consider a return volley of physical violence. But I am old and not skilled in martial arts. And he probably has a hammer in the purse hanging from his shoulder.

"Finally, the snarky comments are too much, and I give up, closing my book of songs. I pack my trumpet in its case. Music doesn't take me back in time, rather it leaves me stranded, knee deep in a humiliating present.

"Later that night I found out the heckler's whole story from the bartender across the street. Heckle Guy had had a sex change operation.

Heckle Guy was in fact Heckle Gal and she had met an Internet date at the bar. The date decided he'd made a mistake and left. She stayed behind, angry for not passing the audition, drinking heavily, threatening everyone in the bar with sexual violence, until the bartender tossed her out. Had I known the heckler's true story, I would not have felt so self-conscious about my musical abilities. The heckler's pain was much worse than mine.

"So you see, Son, don't worry about the judges at your All State audition. They aren't what they seem. They may look tough and sound menacing, but metaphorically, they are really just lonely people suffering from society's inability to accept their new surgically enhanced sexual identities."

My stretched metaphor prompted a good laugh from my son. That evening he practiced his scales with renewed vigor.

My son didn't pass the All State audition. But he's not upset. He is looking forward to auditioning again next year.

My ego recovered from the heckler's abuse, and, trumpet in hand, I am back on Krog Street, playing old tunes for a new audience.

Dorothy leaves Kansas and she returns.

Odysseus leaves Penelope and because he returns we have the *Odyssey*.

Try to leave Earth. Once you reach escape velocity, where are you going to go? Halley's comet travels in circles. Sooner or later the whole universe will reduce itself to its origins, a tiny dot of matter, which explodes in a flash of light and starts the cycle all over again.

So go ahead, listen to that inner voice urging you to move on, open that door and leave. But don't fool yourself. Sooner or later, you'll be back.

Cast your totally uncountable vote for the winner:

☐ LEAVE: Bobbin Wages

☐ RETURN: Bill Taft

WORK

vs

PLAY

WORK: Josh Zagoren

Don't play with me.

Why would you? Playing with something is to probe it, curiously explore it, fiddle with it, manhandle and to operate without knowledge. To play with something, with someone, with yourself is for yourself, by yourself and serves no other purpose but your own selfish needs. So don't play with me. Because it's not about me, it's about you and that's rude, son. Why would you play with something when you could learn how to WORK it? What good does it do the world if all we do is play with things — Needling, doodling, sauntering, daydreaming — when you could be the guy who knows how to WORK that thing? That one thing that some people try to work but can't, others gave up, and others still simply don't have the skills you have. You have mad skills! And those skills are mad enough that you know how to WORK that thing. There is no time to waste on this earth, in our lives. We are put here to achieve things and achievement is the only great reward.

Screw that medal. You know how much that medal costs? Not nearly as many hours as it took you to get it. But the fact that you spent your time, your precious, gilded, intricately earned time making yourself the best at the thing you want to be the best at can only be measured by the one who dares to challenge you. And gold medals may be costly, but the work you put in to win one is PRICELESS.

Go ahead and play, relax, amuse, entertain, recreate, fritter and waste the hours in an off-hand way. But know that one day you'll find 10 years have got behind you, no one told you when to run, you missed the starting gun. And if you think I'm just quoting like a snoot with a literary degree, know that last sentence is from a rock song. And by all means, blast your water bong and get ripped but know the men who wrote that song: Roger Waters, David Gilmour, Nick Mason and Richard Wright of the progressive rock band Pink Floyd weren't playing around when they took the time and did the work it took to make that song that you're frying your ass off to, hippie. Get a job. Work for it and then you can sit back and bask in the glory of knowing that you made something the has sold 40 million copies and counting since its release in 1973 and has since gone on to be selected for preservation in the United States National Recording Registry by the Library of Congress for being deemed "culturally, historically, or aesthetically significant" and any stinky, hairy, stoner human being that was farted on to this planet can play it, but you worked to make it.

You're right, it's late, it's after five, time to chill out. That's the secret to living longer isn't it? Chilling out. So mellow man, slow your roll, hang with your buds, chug some brews, seeing how fast you can down that red plastic cup of PBR. But unless you're Steven Petrosino from Carslisle, PA, you're just being cute. Steven Petrosino chugged 1 liter of beer in 1.3 seconds, brah, that's the WORLD RECORD brah. And 1 liter is 33 ounces, that's 2 pints brah, that's 4 cups in 1.3 seconds brah. Now tell me you'll never have to use math brah.

You're right — so what? You can do that.

No you can't.

If you wanted to do that you'd have to give up the adorable unicorn fantasy tale that you can get things just by doing them or being drunk enough. You have to work to earn that glory. What good is living forever if you never did anything?

Let's try a different game: Anyone can catch a grape in their mouth. Takes a second, just do it. But can you catch one in the air from 327 feet and 6 inches? If you can, then you beat Paul Tavilla from the United States of America and you would hold the Guinness World Record for grape catching. Ask Adam Winrich from Eau Claire, Wisconsin how much fun he's having with his bullwhip, and he'll laugh derisively in your chubby pink cheeks and tell you it's a lot more fun to hold the world record for most bullwhip cracks in one minute, and then he'll do it 257 times for you, one-handed. 'Cause he knows how big boy pants fit. He knows if you're gonna whip anything out, you better know how to WORK it.

But yeah you're right, we should all just calm down and play some music, it's cool. Oh you have a drum set? Sweet. You wanna jam? Can you jam 1208 beats in one minute? No you can't because you're name isn't Tom Grosset. I don't even know what your name is, but have fun *playing* the drums.

Anything that's worth anything is worth the work. And I know what you're going to say: Work isn't fun. Don't we all wish everyday could be a day on the playground: somersaulting, hopscotching, pogo-sticking, sack racing, hula hoop racing, pogo balling, egg and spoon racing, stilt walking, frog jumping, bat balancing, see sawing, tiddlywinking, blowing balloons, pushing oranges with our noses, catching pancakes, piggyback running, blowing peas, reading poetry, balancing shit on our chins and eating mashed potatoes? Yep sounds like a blast.

But unless your name is Ashrita Furman and you did all of those plus 501 other things better than the population of this planet so many times that you hold the Guinness World record for most world records, then you're just playin' around.

PLAY: Cullen Crawford

It seems the thing to do here would be obvious. Simply show up, not get too drunk, and rail against work to a jury of people who, on a Tuesday night, gathered at a bar called The Hideout, which sounds like a 10 year old named it. To sell the idea that the convivial, the boisterous, the fun is somehow better than the soul-dredging, wrinkle-farm shit-buffet of late capitalism.

But here's the thing: I like work.

Work conjures sweaty overalls tossed in a pile next to a lunch pail; big, rusty American hands pouring glowing liquid metal into a dirty trough while sparks fall in the background and Bruce Springsteen buys a reasonably priced late-model pickup truck from a Polish family. Work says that by some noble alchemy, you can add sweat to nothing and get a goddamn something. And that, pals, is an attractive notion.

And then we have play. Play is many things: most of them asinine. It is Wrigleyville and James Franco. It's a Mazda Miata. Play is horse ownership or an adult man wearing shorts. Play is the Dartmouth University Improv Team "Casual Thursday," a real thing that I looked up and is real. In a world with the wolf at one door and the rag and bone man at the other, play is, in a word, irresponsible. At least for those of a certain station. Yeah, I'm making this a class thing.

Because you know who isn't grossed out by the word "play?" The malignant rich: Investment bankers who call their Lamborghinis "toys". Monstrous men and their skeletal wives tooling around the Hamptons in one of those motorboats that's all shiny and wooden. While they are wintering in wherever and running off to the Orient on a lark and ruining New York simply by trying to enjoy it. You and me and all the other dead-eyed peasants are spouting the virtue of a good day's work.

Also, I know it's insulting to both of us that I should even have to say this but: play is fun... Ok, seriously, as much as it makes me feel like Jimmy Buffett giving the commencement address at Coconut

Brother's Tropical Clown College, let's do it. Let's explore the ways that play is better than work. I submit to you the following list of things; some of which happen at work and some at play. See if you can guess which is which.

A little boy, too shy to ever speak in class, feels like the most powerful, indestructible being in Christendom because he's holding a stick that isn't a stick but a gleaming sword made of light, sizzling with the blood of those who might hurt him.

- A woman with a B.A. in philosophy has until 3:30 to finish an online questionnaire to prove she understands not to molest her coworkers.

- A confused and angry thirteen year old, alone in the basement, wet with rage and acne, pounds out a guitar riff that feels like firing a gun right into god's eye.

- A middle-aged woman slowly and calmly explains to you that the reason you messed up her latte is the same reason your race will never make it in this world.

- A guy enjoys soccer.

- A cinderblock falls off the roof of a worksite and kills a man before he ever gets to see the face of his unborn son.

- Anyone smiles ever.

- A man gets a memo asking employees to please not eat lunch on the toilet. (That one is real and it happened to me.)

I would say, "you do the math" but that would be work and fuck work.

And, look, maybe play isn't so puerile or feckless after all. I mean, Casual Thursday aside: Play is how Bach and Benjamin Franklin and John fucking Cleese plumbed up ideas that sent people into varying degrees of uproar. Play is how adorable tiger babies learn to rip the hot, wet throats out of anything that can feel pain.

And play is defiant. Playing is macho, goddammit. To play is to look into the face of this random, violent, glue factory of a universe and say, "I feel like I haven't ridden enough roller coasters lately."

It's Carl Sandburg's Hungarians drinking by the river.

It's Mercutio cracking hilarious one-liners even as he bleeds to death on the pavement.

It's Xenon the rockstar bounty hunter and his space-dog sidekick visiting the pleasure domes in this science-fiction screenplay I'm currently writing.

So toil your hearts out. And put pride in your work and all that other bullshit.. Because, yes, work is wholesome and purifying, and it's driving the engines of commerce — even if that engine's being revved by the one percent, doing donuts in the crumbling parking lot of the free market. But, ever since our simian ancestors made the colossal fuck-up of evolving brains capable of anything more than hunger and breathing, play is essential. These brains that invented hammers and atom bombs and the Slap Chop (the amazing slicing chopping and dicing tool that makes cooking a dream); these brains also invented Go-Karts, and puzzles, and Improv at Dartmouth University because we needed something to keep us from murdering ourselves with our Slap Chops.

So I say to you take play back from those prep-school Ayn Rand-shaped dildos. No more cringing at the word "play". Play. Play with your kids or your video games, or your significant other's throbbing swimsuit area and leave your shit at the office even when you think you shouldn't.

Because, ladies and gentlemen, I envy my opponent. All he has to do is stand up here and sell you an idea that has already been sold to you and yours a thousand times over since the first man in charge said the words "Divine Right of Kings": That work is your lot in life and you are lucky to have it. However I am tasked to somehow convince you, and myself, of a thing which life, our betters, and the universe at large has gone to inconceivable pains to contradict: that we deserve more. That all our hobbies and hopeless crushes, and secret, nagging fucking unkillable dreams aren't shameful guilty pleasures. That they are, in fact, what's coming to you.

Cast your totally uncountable vote for the winner:

☐ WORK: Josh Zagoren

☐ PLAY: Cullen Crawford

FANTASY

VS

REALITY

FANTASY: Gwynedd Stuart

If you ever utilize Google to find the best fantasy books of all time, there is a 100 percent chance you'll happen upon bestfantasybooks.com, a website that specializes in producing subjective lists of the best fantasy books by sub-genre, along with long-winded analyses of each book's whimsical, *majikal* merits.

There's a list of the best fantasy books for women, the best fantasy books for children, the best romance fantasy books, the best vampire romance books, the best sword and sorcery books...

... and then there's a list entitled "worst fantasy books ever". Not of any particular sub-genre. Just the worst overall.

The website's moderator — a person who's spent "20 or so years devouring fantasy books," and probably about as many years wondering why he can't have a decent bowel movement — explains, "To make this list, the book must REALLY be a steaming pile of donkey defecation. Think of this list as those books you should not read... NOT EVEN IF SOMEONE HOLDS A GUN TO YOUR HEAD."

The occupant of the number-one spot on the list isn't a book, but a man, an author whose entire fantasy catalogue has been deemed donkey doody by a self-proclaimed authority on the subject. The author's name is Robert Stanek.

In the interest of time, here's an abridged version of what the site says about Stanek:

One word: avoid!

(I love when things start that way because of course the one word is followed lots and lots of other words. Anyway.)

There's a saying "don't judge a book by the cover," but in the case of a Robert Stanek novel, you should judge by the cover. My blind niece could do a better job making book covers than that.

[His books] evince all the skill of an adolescent girl, writing her first creative piece on a prancing pony. Keep away from his books

if you value your sanity. His prose is so bad your eyes will bleed.

Stanek wins The Best Fantasy Books award for being the worst fantasy author and writing the worst fantasy novels. In fact, I'll go one further. Stanek is not just a bad fantasy writer, he's the nemesis of the fantasy world, the Dark Lord of fantasy authors. Please, if you see a Robert Stanek novel, run like hell because you're risking your literary soul.

My interest, it was piqued. Not enough to read anything Robert Stanek has written, but enough to Google his name some more and read the other mean things people have written about him. After a little more research, I decided that Robert Stanek is number 1 on my list of people who are great. That list appears on my new website peoplewhoaregreat.com.

Some background: Stanek is a Desert Storm vet and family man whose 70-entry bibliography includes the "Ruin Mist" series, "The Kingdoms and the Elves of the Reaches" — books one through four — and *Windows 7: The Definitive Guide.* His full name is William Robert Stanek, which allows fans like me to lovingly refer to him as "Billy Bob." He writes fantasy as Robert, but writes books on computer software and business composition as William — and I'd be very interested to learn amount the decision making process there. "Robert just sounds more... magical," is how I imagine it going.

Other things about Billy Bob: It's widely believed that he writes positive Amazon reviews about his own books. He's also sent a fake cease-and-desist order from a fake lawyer to a real fanzine that questioned the legitimacy of all his positive Amazon reviews. His books are all self published. And there's a decent amount of evidence to suggest that he Photoshopped himself into a picture alongside legitimate fantasy author and old-man Bryan Cranston look-alike, Brian Jakes.

On his personal website, Stanek posted an interview conducted by someone called Dave Brubaker. (If the interview was printed any place other than Robertstanek.com, he doesn't say.) The first question Brubaker asks: "What do you say to those who are calling you the

Tolkien for the new millennium?" The only reference to Stanek being compared to Tolkien that I found online was an Amazon review — one that appeared to have been taken down — written by Dave Brubaker. Who bestfantasybooks.com would probably suggest is actually Robert Stanek.

You know, forget Stanek's lack of talent and professional scruples — I think everyone's thinking about his work and his image in a way that doesn't exhibit much creativity.

I'd like to read you an email I wrote to bestfantasybooks.com in defense of Stanek. It's written from the perspective of a Stanek fan... who is actually Stanek.

Dearest Sir or Madam,

A fine day in Middle Earth, isn't it? LOL. I'm just fucking with you.

I'm writing to formally take issue with your scathing and potentially harmful review of the works of Robert Stanek, a man many call the "Tolkien of the new millennium." I've also heard him called "J.K. Rowling, but with a wand and a couple of huge sorcerers' stones." Again, LOL.

First, I'd like to say I'm sorry to hear about your niece. Blindness is an unfortunate affliction, and I admire the pluck she's shown by continuing to illustrate book covers. Maybe she'd like to draw one for Mr. Stanek one day? The ball, as they say, is in your court.

As a fellow devourer of fantasy fiction — nom nom nom — I'm surprised you don't see the post-modern complexity of Robert Stanek's life and work. Don't you see? By writing his own glowing book reviews, calling himself a best-selling author, and electronically pasting his visage into photos with other authors, Stanek is, with a stroke of his mighty pen, WRITING HIS OWN FANTASY. He's Tolkien, but he's also Frodo Fucking Baggins — you catch my drift? IT'S BRILLIANT.

But in the words of the great George R.R. Martin, "Haters gonna hate."

Love in magic,

Billy Bob Brubaker

REALITY: Bernard Setaro Clark

To begin with, I don't believe in God. That's not to say that I'm an atheist, because I'm not. I don't disbelieve in God. That would require more ideological commitment than I possess. I simply refuse to actively believe in him. I used to call myself an agnostic, but I felt that label lacked panache. These days, if anybody asks, I refer to myself as an existential humanist. Don't bother asking me what that means. I am not going to explain it to you. I'm not here to convert. What does this have to do with *Reality* you might be wondering?

Well, I wasn't always a non-believer, you see. I was born and raised Catholic. Baptized and confirmed. In fact, when I was very young, I used to pray to God. I prayed all the time. I didn't just pray, I had long, in-depth conversations with God in my head much like I am talking to you right now.

You see, I was never completely alone. No matter what went on in my life, no matter how shitty or awesome things got, I always had this friend, this father figure, this all-knowing, all-seeing, all-loving deity hanging out with me, just outside my awareness. Sort of like having a mute Jewish Viking superhero as an imaginary friend.

Now I'm not going to go into the whys and hows of my loss of faith. I simply don't have that kind of time. Let's just say that I still have some probing questions about the Crusades and leave it at that.

What I will tell you is that in the absence of God, a writhing hunger to experience the Truth of existence remained. A yearning for Gnosis if you will. In pursuit of Gnosis, I have traversed some rather strange landscapes. I have dabbled in Zen Buddhism, studied Qaballah, practiced Magick with a K, apprenticed as a shaman, and entertained the notion that I may or may not have communicated psychically with a vast super-intelligent astral spider-god while on a Herculean amount of drugs.

What? Oh, like you haven't?

Philip K. Dick, a famous dead science fiction writer said, "Reality is that which, when you stop believing in it, does not go away."

Now, at this point, I'm sure some of you see where I'm going with this. Especially those of you that do, in fact, believe in some deity or higher power.

You're thinking "Oh, he's going to talk about how when he stopped believing in God, that he lost that sense of presence he'd always known and suddenly felt loss and loneliness in an uncaring universe with only his own thoughts and a vague sense of horror to keep him company and since God went away so easily when he stopped believing in him then according to that Dick fellow God must not be real."

You would, of course, be wrong.

I'm simply stating that over the course of my lifetime, I have experienced a multiplicity of Realities, all of which seemed quite valid at the time.

Indulge me for a moment. I would like those of you who believe in God to look around the room, right now and try to make eye contact with those of you that do not believe in God. Go on don't be shy. We're all friends here.

Recognize that the person with whom you are currently sharing an uncertain yet meaningful glance, does not exist in the same Reality that you do. In fact, due to the limitations of a uniquely subjective consciousness, the permutations of biology and the mechanics of four-dimensional space-time, you do not exist in the same Reality as any other person in this room.

Several of you think I am full of shit. Don't play. I know who you are. I can see it in your faces. You're thinking, "Shit is real, you're an idiot for saying otherwise, let me punch you in the face to prove it."

Oh, really?

According to science, more than 99 percent of all matter, including your body, is made up of empty space. That's not even cutting edge, all right? That's from shit they came up with in the 1930s.

The really cutting edge shit, the shit with math that makes your head explode — and I mean actually blows up a person's head (it is the number-one cause of death among quantum physicists) — that shit: quantum foam, super-symmetrical strings, parallel universes?... If that shit is to be believed then all that crazy sci-fi shit we've all read about and seen in movies, time travel, teleportation, faster-than-light travel, all that shit may actually see the light of day. So I don't even want to hear any whining about, "But I'm real. I'm right here. I can prove I exist by making noise and stuff."

At this point, I'm not even fucking sure if I'm real!

The bottom line is that there is an awful lot of disagreement about what this Reality thing is in the first place. Right now, this very moment, people in the world are killing other people because they don't agree on the nature of Reality. My God is better than your God. My skin is better than your skin. In whom and in what orifice I like to put my penis is better than where you put yours. It seems to me that most people are just looking for a Reality in which their lives don't suck.

The problem is that we think we all live in the same Reality, but there is no consensus. For every worldview, there are at least two others in direct opposition to yours. And everybody thinks that their version of Reality is The One.

Well, I say don't let someone else dictate your Reality. Define your Reality your own damn selves. You're doing it anyway whether you realize it or not. Own it. Take control.

Robert Anton Wilson said, "Reality is what you can get away with."

Well? What are you getting away with? What are *YOU* getting away with?

Oh, I nearly forgot. I'm supposed to be defending Reality against its Arch-Nemesis, Fantasy. Well, I suppose some of you did come to see some literary blood spilled. So here goes... ignoring the fact that Fantasy is an artifact of Human Consciousness and that Human Consciousness is contained within Reality (*Reality wins*) and ignoring the fact that Consciousness may actually dictate Reality making Fantasy nothing more than Unrealized Potential Reality (*Reality wins again*) I just gotta ask one question, and please feel free to recontextualize this question according to your own personal sexual preference:

Which is more appealing, the blow job you're getting in your mind's eye, or the blow job you're actually getting?

Cast your totally uncountable vote for the winner:

☐ FANTASY: Gwynedd Stuart

☐ REALITY: Bernard Setaro Clark

PROSE

VS

POETRY

Editors' note:

This bout took place at the Poetry Foundation in Chicago.

PROSE: Diana Slickman

You might, if you are a person of a compassionate disposition or a squeamish nature, you might be feeling sorry for me right about now. To have to endorse prose, to champion it in a contest against poetry here in the very seat of poetry's power, may appear to you to be a pitiable task, a fool's errand.

But am I intimidated by poetry's home field advantage?

Am I reluctant to be a heretic, here, in the temple of poetry?

Am I afraid to speak truth to power?

No, sir or madam; no I am not.

Look, let's not fool around. When you have something to say, come right on out and say it. Lay it out there plain. Don't be coy and don't get fancy. Employ no metrical feet; omit rhyme schemes. Avoid alliteration, elision, assonance. Eschew clever punctuation and irregular line breaks. Put it in a paragraph! A complete paragraph with full, grammatical sentences! Write it in prose.

You want a solid line of words right across the page from one margin to the next. You don't need poetry with its yawning expanses of white space, reproaching you for the waste of good paper. If you're going to cut down a tree (a tree which is more lovely than any poem), pulp it, press it, and cut it into sheets to write on, you better make it worth that tree's life. You'd better use that paper up. Use the whole damned page. Don't just sprinkle ideas on there like little candied violets. Fill that sucker with ideas. Use prose!

But I like poetry, you say. Forgive me but that's bullshit. You *think* you like poetry. You think you're *supposed* to like poetry. You think people will look down on you for *not* liking poetry. You go digging around for poems maybe once or twice a year, when someone gets married or you have to placate a child. Mostly, you ignore its very existence. But everybody likes prose! Really likes it! Everybody uses it, everybody reads it, every damned day. It's everywhere.

If you want to look at this from a purely economic perspective

– and because this is America we are practically constitutionally required to look at it that way, whether *you* want to or not – prose is the clear winner. Despite appearances, the ostensible success of the practice that is on display here at the Poetry Foundation, poetry doesn't pay. It isn't economically viable, despite its economy of language. The supply of poetry outstrips the demand about, oh, I don't know, 10,000 fold? So great is the surplus that they are, in fact, *giving it away*. Poetry has to be subsidized by wealthy eccentrics and charitable institutions just to keep its metaphorical lights on. There is no Prose Foundation. You know why? It doesn't need the help. Prose sells! Comparatively well!

And that's because prose is useful and ubiquitous; it's prosaic, after all. Why deny it? There's no shame in being common and straightforward, no shame in being effective and necessary. *No shame!* Prose is the unromantic workhorse of ideas. It carries meaning across the gulf between us like a freighter: a big, solid, sea-worthy conveyance. And like such vessels, it can be beautiful and majestic, awesome, weighty, the smoke of ideas pouring from its stacks. Prose easily carries any kind of cargo. Nothing is too base or too delicate to be stowed in its hold. Raw materials, finished products, instruction, myth, law, memory, humor, a million ideas. You name it, prose will bring it safely to you. To *you*, no matter who you are. If you can read, the good ship prose will bring you whatever you need with a minimum of fuss. But poetry... poetry is like a clown on a unicycle carrying a single glass of Pernod, balanced atop a mirrored ball. Inefficient and impractical, it's not for everybody and often way more trouble than it is worth.

Everything poetry can do, prose can do. Just more effectively. And there is so much that poetry, god love it, just cannot do. Science, medicine, government, love. Yes, love – the favorite stomping ground of poetry – love is better served by prose. Prose is a hot, hard, wet kiss on the mouth. It can mean any number of things but there's no question that you've been kissed. Poetry is a veiled look from behind a lace fan across a darkened room. You're not sure what the message is or if it's even directed at you. It might lust or it might be contempt. Maybe it's near-sightedness. Could be anything. And while you're trying to figure out what poetry is getting at, prose and I have come to an understanding, gone home, had great, deeply meaningful sex, followed by beer and a sandwich, and have fallen asleep, satisfied.

Look, I don't hate poetry. Poetry's good. Poetry's fine. It has its place. This place. And I'm not saying prose is everything to everyone. Just 98 percent of everything to everyone. And by everyone I mean you. You. You who chose to come here tonight. Not to a poetry slam. Not to a poetry reading. To a prose reading.

POETRY: J.W. Basilo

Audience Note: I stand before you, charged with the task of writing in defense of poetry, an epic 7–minute Ars Poetica if you will, because Belknap is trying to set a trap wherein I write prose about poetry in the very building that poetry built, along with very large donations from people who don't call what I do poetry. The irony here, not lost on me. Why are you trying to make me look like a punk, Ian? I never write in the Ars Poetica because it's always felt like pleasuring myself to a pornographic video starring me. But alas, I am happy to oblige.

Poetry: the word itself a stand-in, a metaphor for beauty
The sway and line of the body in perfect congruence with the sonata
      (The sonata itself, poetry)
The way a moment seems to hang itself in space, gilded frame
gorgeous.
A wisp of hair swaying across an eye, like love announcing
      itself through a broken window
Poetry: the act of saying as much as humanly possible in as few
words,
distilling a thunderstorm into a thimble
Poetry: I hate you right now.
      What am I doing here?

Once I was a bartender, hollering myself purple in a dark stockroom,
pulling syllables from the gurgle of a bottleneck.
Not a beverage napkin or empty cigarette pack went unscribbled,
not a single fuck was given
This, the decade of the late night, of the ink blot solace,
of the crimson eyes at dawn because there were more words
waiting in line

There was always another stage, another microphone

another hotspark idea
another bus ride, couch surf, happy
drink sling, bottle hum, iron throw — no matter
drug fingers across clouds like top of a pie
hot throat belt
all night solo mission coffee
run knees napalm sticky
sober couch talk, closer
chest core supernova
wrong turn Indiana, hands held over console, all a metaphor
young dumb brilliant
arms open
       Dear Universe thank you
what happened?

Now:
bed trench, shades drawn glutton
head cloud closed loop feedback
fat liver fat gut groan
arm cross finger point
lip stitch phone booth glass box
Poetry: I hate-respect you

At least you're not prose
Poetry: the only rule is don't suck whilst trying to avoid cliché
       (and even that one, debatable)
perfect for an errant rule snubber, can't no one tell me shit
Watch me make up my own words, watch me say *fizzlecrack*
Watch me hill roll dusk hallelujah
tongue flap grateful

Since feeling is first who cares about the syntax of things?
Watch me quote e.e. cummings, Mr. Perez,
9th grade English Teacher at the high school where I failed

Creative Writing and then got paid to teach Creative Writing
Watch cummings never capitalize or punctuate shit and be canonized
    Try that, with your novels
Watch me say

            stargaze birdsong reckless, marching crosshairs fixed on
further
to a classroom full of students from the parts of the city
    called: roll up your windows and hope no one saw,
with too few desks and no air conditioning,
their brains splintering as to what the hell that means.
Watch their collective jaw drop when I say,
        You're all correct and I'm not sure either, but don't you feel
something?
Half my students can't spell "simile" but they can pull a poem
out of that classroom stench turn your spine to broken glass.

You tell a sledge swing not to split your whole gut in two,
tell 'em stanza break, be wild, write the whole thing backwards if
you're feeling it
Try that, Associated Press, dough rollers at the Panty Waist Patisserie
    (Alliteration, metaphor, boom.)
                (Onomatopoeia)
Pantoum, villanelle, ghazal, sonnet:
lovers I could spend a lifetime learning,
how each rolls inside my hand, on my tongue

Mr. and Mrs. Prose in ratty bathrobes avoid eye contact
over stale coffee, morning after their monthly missionary coitus
Isn't monogamy until we're dead wonderful, dear?
Let us display our passion and call up a murder of smug intern copy editors
chewing their faces and argue the rules of the serial comma

2

It's a canto now, because I said so

3
if I am to sit and sift this world through words
how is it all not a poem:
the sounds and sight and smell of it,
each a story deserving a heightened tongue.

Last week, in the barber chair: the clippers humming their shark
tooth song
with the bachata bark of the broken speaker overhead,
the paleta pusher outside, feet hushing in time with the cart's bells.

Last night, the collapse in my chest
when I finally make my friend's infant daughter laugh
How it always feels in a hospital waiting room

How are these all not poems?
Why would I waste a single word?

Cast your totally uncountable vote for the winner:

[ ] PROSE: Diana Slickman

[ ] POETRY: J.W. Basilo

FULL

VS

EMPTY

FULL: Dani Herd

Medicating with fast food is the Herd family way of life. We celebrate with food, and we mourn with food. The beginning of every new college year was signaled by a trip with my mom to the Moe's over on Ponce. When Chris Peckron broke up with me the summer before tenth grade, my dad didn't say a word, but drove straight to Waffle House and brought me back a slice of chocolate pie. When I was rejected from the eighth grade girls' basketball team, my mom ventured to Taco Bell for me. Love will always taste like a chicken quesadilla and a Mountain Dew Code Red to me. House Herd is held together by breading and batter and those little crackly bits that fall off the fish at Long John Silver's.

Not-especially-healthy foodstuffs have been staples of my family life for as long as I can remember. Which is why it came as such a surprise when, in the midst of my senior year at college, my dad told me that I needed to lose at least 20 pounds.

"You need to lose at least 20 pounds." Despite this being the most hurtful thing my father had ever said to me, I actually heard the love in his voice. No particular gender or age or race or anything has a monopoly on body image issues. Back in his high school days, my dad was the Georgia state mile champion. Running long distance every day permitted him to eat whatever he wanted. Until he couldn't, but he did anyway.

Perhaps the appropriate thing for me would have been to seize upon this moment of quasi-vulnerability and attempt to bond with my dad. Come together over the shock of leaving high school athletics and teenage metabolisms behind, but clinging to consistent French fry intake. But I was angry. Not even as much for suggesting that something was wrong with my physical appearance, but for so boldly rejecting what I had come to understand as our way of life. What he himself had taught me! I was distraught every single day back then, and definitely not hiding it especially well. What was I supposed to do besides eat? My father's words stung because in them was the complete absence of understanding or at least recognition and curiosity of what was really going on with me.

What was really going on was that I was, as so many tragic heroines are, painfully and entirely in love with someone who did not love me back. He had loved me for a little while, defying our ten-year age difference and some occasional international long distance. When he wanted out, but continued to sleep with me, all I decided to hear was: "If you make yourself someone I like better, I'll add love back into this equation." And so re-achieving this man's love became the primary reason for existence. I breathed and ate and slept and attended class and wracked my brain for ways to become a girl that he could love again. Where I am devoid of good judgment and self-preservation, I am full to bursting with determination.

So, how could I explain to my father that I couldn't possible even consider losing 20 pounds when I was fighting for the affections of a man who absolutely could not resist my round stomach?

Yeah. So, Not-Boyfriend had a thing for curves. And as I had left high school behind and invited some particular softness to my tall frame, I was, shall we say, his type. I knew that my body was a weakness for him, so I wielded it like a soft, pale, fleshy weapon. There was nothing chaste about the way he cupped and clutched my exposed stomach. So exposed it was. Shirts that no longer sat particularly maidenly upon my curvy torso made frequent appearances when we would meet up for what he surely intended to be a platonic friends' hangout. I'd catch his eyes fall upon the swell of my breasts or on a sliver of bare belly, and knew that I had won.

My round, squishy body was the only aspect of mine I was confident he liked, despite his affirmations of my non-physical qualities. He didn't want to date me anymore, but he sure did care about me. He wanted to do what was right and spare me permanent damage. And maybe there's an alternate version of this story where I allow love to transmogrify itself into something healthy and non-sexual and deep, but I wasn't ready to quit trying. Losing 20 pounds would have left me without my only advantage. My roundness was my only source of power over him.

The shame and the sadness and the desperation I felt were all the excuses I needed to indulge in the food that had comforted me since childhood. What I did wasn't ever "emotional eating." No, I was an entitlement eater. I was sad, so I deserved, for example, Chick-fil-A. Most of my Saturday nights in college saw me taking MARTA from my part-time box office job back to my apartment in Decatur. Getting home close to nine on a Saturday night all but guaranteed that my apartment was empty, my roommates having found something fun and age-appropriate to do. It would have been easy to text them and find them and join in the revelry. But despite my overwhelming loneliness, I longed for when the apartment was empty and no one was around to see how truly in need of help I was. My date on these Saturday nights was a spicy chicken sandwich, adorned with waffle fries, a side of ranch and a medium Dr. Pepper.

The real comfort of fast food is in the transaction. Yes, I am aware that money is changing hands in these scenarios. BUT. I am allowed to ask a person for a thing I really want and they will just give it to me. I do not have to cry or plead or promise to do better next time or offer to change myself or put on a desperate happy face. I will ask them for a spicy chicken sandwich, medium fries, a side of ranch and a medium Dr. Pepper and they will let me have it. He or she will place food in a bag for me and they will put that bag in my hand and they may even smile at me and maybe that is enough like love.

After finishing every bite and then using my finger to sop up every lingering smudge of buttermilk ranch, I'd be alone again. At a complete loss for how to feel happy or safe. My belly swollen with fried chicken and utter self-hatred. Physical fullness didn't soothe me. And emotionally, I felt nauseous every day. I was filled to the brim with every feeling that had ever existed. I woke up full of sadness and then felt full of anger at myself for caring so much about whether this man loved me and then full of a confident joy because, "Fuck it, I don't need anyone to validate my existence, right?" and then full of an intoxicating hope when this man sent me a text message and then sad again when the texting died down for the morning and then full of worry about never being enough for anyone, including myself.

Within an hour, I'd be ready to return to bed, exhausted from the intense emotions battling for dominance in my brain. Shortly after a particularly confusing and sweet visit to my apartment that included a gifting of a pint of Ben & Jerry's and a morose sexual encounter, Not-Boyfriend told me that I was a burden and put an end to our communication. As tears streamed down my face, a knot in my stomach undid itself. What I had needed all along was to be finally and completely told "no". Suddenly I was free to think about something else. There was a hole in my life, yes, but also the ability to go out and fill it with anything new.

Fullness is comfortable and safe. For years, I was stuffed. I was a suitcase that needed to be body slammed over and over again to fit all its contents. Barely held together and with my innards haphazardly jumbled. For what it's worth, these days, my dad tells me almost every time he sees me that I've lost weight and look slender. And my satisfaction is not in his approval, but in the merciful realization that I just don't care. Being thin has no impact on my fullness. To be full is to be enough. To be taking up as much physical, mental and emotional space in the world as is allotted to me, no more and no less, and by decree of no one but me.

EMPTY: Cris Gray

The sound of gunfire from one of the neighboring buildings jolts me awake. It doesn't sound real filtered through the speaker of my sleeping pod. It's as if I've fallen asleep with my entertainment monitor on only to be woken by an old war movie. I hear some muffled shouting, screaming and then silence. Gunfire isn't an uncommon sound anymore. I won't be able to go back to sleep now. I flip a switch and the internal LED lights of my artificial cocoon rise to brightness. The inside of my pod is a little bigger than a twin bed and is the closest most come to having their own room. If I had more money, I'd rent something larger. Most couples combine their income and rent one the size of a queen bed to share. I'm not in a couple. I'm as single as they come.

I sit up. The concave ceiling is just tall enough for me to sit upright without bumping my head. A touchscreen on the surface to my right displays 4:35 a.m. I swipe the glowing screen to eject from my tiny chamber. The coffin top silently rises. The left wall lowers like an automated oven door. I swing my legs over and sit on the edge looking out at the large floor-to-ceiling window in front of me. My pod is at the far of end of what used to be an old hotel room. Above me, another pod is supported by a metal support scaffold. The room is dark and silent though eight of us live here in this small tenement. I turn to look at the three other bunk-bed-style stacks of large, metallic eggs. Two sets of two on opposite sides of the square room. My seven roommates are silently sleeping in these soundproof vessels like a barracks of vampire soldiers. Flanking both sides of each egg bunk are two tall storage lockers for the occupants. A small bathroom is at the opposite end of the room by the front door. I try to imagine what it would be like to have this room all to myself. One person in an area that now houses eight is a luxury that only the wealthy can afford.

I stand up. The exposed concrete floor is cold on my bare feet. I look out at the darkened windows of the building directly across the street. Nothing moves. I glance down at the empty, dimly lit pavement far below and decide to go for a walk to kill the remaining hours before dawn. I enjoy walking in the early morning because the streets are usually empty. It's one of the only times I can be alone and have space to breathe. A stark contrast to the crush of human bodies I experience the rest of the day in this overpopulated city.

It's not just the cities anymore. Everywhere is overpopulated. I turn to my locker and a familiar face looks back at me from the mirror mounted in the door. I grin. The face grins back. "You big dumdum," I say as the face silently mimes my words. Sometimes I can't believe that I've looked at this same face for over two decades. My face has not aged a day since my 40th birthday. I wish this made me unique but it doesn't. We're collectively referred to as Elders. No one in this country over 40 has aged or died of natural causes in over 100 years. Science and medicine have been unable to explain why. The best they could do is narrow the earliest documented occurrence of an Elder to around the year 1900 in Colorado Springs. The old don't die to make room for the young here. Grandparents, great grandparents and almost everyone born since the 20th century still walks around. They're all here taking up what is now extremely valuable space.

It's 2025 and there are more than 3 billion Americans living on Earth. Almost a third of the human race resides on the North American continent. Even with the expansion into the Canadian and Mexican states, there isn't enough room. The young compete with Elders for basic resources. Jobs, apartments, even food. The Elders obviously have the upper hand. Many have acquired more wealth and decades of experience simply because they've been here longer. Children of the wealthy Elders have some advantage, but they have little chance of ever receiving inheritances unless their rich, semi-immortal parents meet their demise through dubious circumstances.

I enter a code into the locker keypad and it slides open, revealing only one set of clothes, a worn pair of boots, a jacket, and a newly purchased six-pack of socks inside. I pull on the jeans and button up the shirt. Sitting on the edge of the open pod, I slide my feet into the warm socks followed by the heavy boots. I zip on the black field jacket I got from a military surplus shop. The locker automatically locks as I close the door. I touch the AWAY button on the pod's exterior control screen and it transforms back into its original egg shape.

I exit the room and the heavy metal door closes and locks behind me before I shuffle down the hallway toward the bank of elevators. As I exit the building into the street, the cold air instantly turns my breath into white smoke. I light a cigarette, take a long drag and exhale another plume of white vapor that is no longer carcinogenic to me. Gripping the cigarette between my teeth, I pull a wool cap from my coat pocket and slide it over my head. Two police cars speed by with their blue strobe lights beating the quiet air like hummingbird wings made of nothing but light. They converge two blocks away joining another car outside a building. I thrust my cold hands into the soft, warm lining of the field jacket pockets. The knuckles of my right hand bump against the grip of the hidden EM pistol. I look towards the blue lights and then in the opposite direction down the quiet sidewalk. I take a few steps and stop.

"Aw, shit. Whatcha gonna do, ya big dum-dum? Live forever?" I say to nobody. I turn and walk towards the flashing lights, curiosity now outweighing that previous desire to be alone on these empty streets.

Cast your totally uncountable vote for the winner:

☐ FULL: Dani Herd

☐ EMPTY: Cris Gray

TOP

vs

BOTTOM

TOP: Colin Iago McCarthy

Tops spin round, and dance a dance, influenced by the stars and the breath that leaves your body. As you breathe the exhalation blends and drifts with the surrounding life, and the top's spinning influences you. As the potential which you drove into the top winds out, and the gyroscopic precession takes hold, the top wobbles, and tumbles, and processes to the ground. This energy, this faltering, this wobbling, this winding, wends its way into our souls, and shows us the way to go. To interact with the tides, to lay claim to the stars, to lay, and lie, and let the stillness of eternity flow through us as the breath goes in and out our bodies, and tumbles this top.

Gyroscopic stability. As creatures anchored to the flow of time, stability is often illusory. And eternity washes past, and sweeps us in its embrace. Swept past the borders we once knew, into a virgin territory, a vast expanse of the unknown, The One thing, and this is it. That thing, that need, that stabilizing catalyst, that gyroscoping tumbler. And we rise to the challenge, and face this new thing, this unknown force, which calls to our hearts, and calls us up, and draws us out. We hear, we answer, and we claw our way through this filtered sea of perception, and stroke our way out, up and up, and finally we are on top, and we can see the vast array of probability. That singularity of possibility, which drives out the "could," allowing only the "is." And not just that, but the "is" which **IS**, that which we know, but which is only one of many, and ours is but the shunted "could" over there, and we will never know, for, surely as we see Time in only one way, our walls of perception keep us hemmed in from over there, and who's to say that you'd even want to go there. A there where all you know is not quite so. Where everything is similar, and off by just a little. A chain hotel in another city, where the art's the same, but the colors are all different. And this is your life, because it is now over there, where all that came before is just a little different, and not quite turned the same way. The spin of each neutrino a wobble off from you, and you sit spinning in the flow that is the new now, and wonder at the gaping, yawning, aching, spawning, wanton want for that other. The piece that, if we had it, could pull us together and create the tight magnificence that is "belong." That whole other whose reflection reflects the beating spin of our own disastrous magnificence, and showers us with the radiant possibilities of now. That Whole whose very presence sets harmonic resonance burning, sparking symphonic glory in our burning hearts, setting our souls alight with a fire unquenched by the daily grind. Unquenched by the shaming fingers of "Can't." Unquenched by Duty's need. The Whole whose sympathetic syncopation sets our spirits free, to soar, secure in the place to land. Secure in the want of another. Secure to seek the fullness every breath promises, and every want steals.

And we remember that which brought us here.

The hunger to be known. A hunger which drives us off every day. A hunger to see, a hunger to taste, a hunger to know. This hunger inside which wants to see the brilliance within reflected back at us from the anima of an Other. This hunger which pulls us to our feet, and makes us put our shoes on, and stride into the night, to this place. Here where we seek the ultimate, here where our hearts can be sated, here where walls can drop and words be said. Here, where meaning is imbued, and every glance and word infused with possibility. Here, where our minds work hard to catch your eye, and our words sound strained, too stretched for beauty's release. Where at the top of our game, we'd bring you to a place where all doubt becomes a shadow, and noonday sun buns away the misting eyes of shame. Where, at the top of our game, we'd send forth your friends, sated by our good intentions, but really hope to just get a real number. Where at the end of the night we might find ourselves with a realm of possibilities opened before us, so that we can move forward with a strength and bravado normally left for the Gods. Where in the 2 o'clock clean-up-kick-out from the bar we wander the streets for home, wishing that the last round hadn't been ours, so that we could pull our dance-tired feet into a cab, and hail ourselves home. Here, where a singularity of possibility opens its great maw to us, and the whole line seems so straight, how could we possibly avoid it, how could we possibly miss it? And how could we want to. This line, this here, where dreams of others come true, and the heartfelt beating pulse under your ribs is driven by the knowledge that there is another. Here, where now my hand is in yours and the way home doesn't seem so far, it could in fact be twice as far as reality, but that wouldn't mind me none, just to have the time to hold you, and have a pocket of IS in this world of could/should, possible/probable, can't/won't. Getting on top of this feeling inside that allows the possible to be, getting on top of this IS that has fused my life so fully that any other could just couldn't, to me. Getting on top of this spinning world of now. And finding myself spinning slowly as you go down on top.

BOTTOM: Joy Carletti

Let's get to the bottom of things, shall we? The nitty-gritty? The meaty underbelly of this whole thing. You're probably curious about how this WRITE CLUB operation works, eh? Here it is: a look behind the mask.

Casey Childers and Steven Westdahl, your SF WRITE CLUB cornermen, talk up this event to all their friends, of course. It should come as no great surprise that they have literary-minded friends, wordsmiths and poets and just those fuckers who sit in the corner of a bar and hold court, telling story after story till the place closes down. Oral tradition as it is today. The word gets put out: writers needed. And lo, we respond.

So a few days after WRITE CLUB May, I got booked officially for this month. The first email that came out told me I was going up against my boyfriend, and that our challenge was Top vs. Bottom. But! It didn't tell us who had which topic.

So I got to start pondering which topic I'd prefer. And it happens, I had a story for Top. It was a good story. It was a story about orgasms. In my mind's eye, I would tell this story, and y'all were going to be left shifting uncomfortably in your seats, adjusting your trousers, and then Colin was going to get up and lay some rhyming couplet shit on you that you wouldn't even be able to process because you would be so blinded by your own boners.

But then the next email came from WRITE CLUB, and as you know, I got bottom.

Bottom.

Bottom.

I was a theatre major. I've seen a lot of Shakespeare and done a lot of Shakespeare and read a lot of Shakespeare — hell, I've even improvised Shakespeare. So, you say "bottom," and I picture a guy with a donkey's head. That's all I see. I was married to a Scotsman for seven years; he always called my ass my "bot-tom", and every time he did… Boom. Guy with a donkey's head. I may even have pictured him with a donkey's head. Too many productions of *A Midsummer Night's Dream* have actively ruined the word "bottom" for me.

But I have to get up here right now and argue *for* bottom. I have to make you vote for bottom. Fuck.

Intellectually, I realize that this should not be a hard sell. This is San Francisco. Bottom. Make a few cheap jokes about the Folsom Street Fair and call it done.

But here's the thing about writer's block. It happens at weird, inconvenient times, and you start doing weird shit to find your way back from it. My first approach? I do a Google image search for bottoms. Not safe for work. And ultimately, not that inspiring.

I check dictionary.com, see if I really know what bottom means. I realize — yes, yes I do.

I make myself a Spotify playlist of bottom songs. And then things start to get truly ugly. Because songs are emotional. And songs with "bottom" in them are just weighted.

And suddenly. Suddenly I'm back in the last year of my marriage, when life started to pile on the shit. When my husband was working extreme hours at his startup, coming home close to midnight, and not really ever talking to me. My job was eight hours a day of mental health insurance scut work, when the most fun part of the day might be talking to a bona fide crazy person on the phone and having them swear at me in some truly creative fashion, and I wasn't allowed to hang up. I was doing an improv show with a group of anti-social perfectionists. I often felt like my only friend was my therapist. I couldn't remember the last time I'd gotten laid.

I *could* remember the last time I'd felt this way. Senior year in college. I'd woken up in the middle of the night and thought I was being stabbed in the chest, only to find myself — surprisingly — alone. I spent the next three weeks in the hospital while they tried to figure out what was wrong, and one hypothesis after another was proved incorrect until finally the bacteria that had been eating my lung the entire time penetrated the lung lining, and the doctors had to go in and remove my upper right lobe. A month later, when I came out of the hospital, the university tried to charge me for the semester because I hadn't dropped my classes quickly enough for their liking. They backed down, but then said since I wasn't registered for classes, my medical insurance wasn't covered. So I had $100,000 in hospital bills. Oh, and I needed to pay for my dorm room. After all, I hadn't moved out before going to the emergency room.

It is a cold, dark place, the bottom. It is a place of tears and hurt and defeat and crushed dreams. But it has its purpose.

When you climb a mountain, you can turn around and bask in the views in all directions. You drink in the wonder around you. But when you are at an emotional low, you pivot, take in your surroundings, and at a certain point in your 360, a pivot in your mind happens as well. But that turn is a 180. Your mind does a sudden what-the-fuck... Because while you can use great height to see a great distance, it takes an emotional valley to achieve true clarity.

On the heels of that bottomed-out clarity comes a resolve unlike anything you can achieve when you're at the top. A resolve that says, I can change my situation. I can change my life. I can change the fucking world.

And the brilliant thing about the bottom is: you're so fucking low: anything can start that pivot. A phone call from a friend that reminds you — there's more to life than just a lung. A sudden random crush that reminds you — a marriage isn't supposed to be just a close friendship. An email from the WRITE CLUB guys that reminds you — you *can* actually write.

And so, I celebrate my bottom. I bless the pivot points in my life that put me in the place that I am now — in a career that I never would have had if I hadn't lost my lung, that features much more human interaction than the one I was planning beforehand. I revel in the pit that ultimately landed me in this phenomenal relationship where — no matter who wins this thing — we're going home and getting laid to celebrate. And I even relish the occasional writer's block that sends me down strange paths like Spotify and dictionary.com, because I do occasionally learn things there.

So bottoms up, people. I have looked at the world from the bottom of a well and this... this fat-bottomed girl has made her rockin' world turn around.

Cast your totally uncountable vote for the winner:

☐ TOP: Colin Iago McCarthy

☐ BOTTOM: Joy Carletti

SMOOTH

vs

ROUGH

SMOOTH: Samantha Irby

1 "i like it smooth," my then-boyfriend announced
leaning to his right to peer over my knees
"ew, i'm a grown lady," was my snotty reply
"and you can't have a forest without a few trees."

2 smooth is for peanut butter, for sailing, for silk
and, if you're boring, smooth is sometimes for jazz
smooth is for lips and for bottoms of babies
but smooth is **not** for the crack of my ass.

3 "i can't see what i'm doing," he whined like a girl
stopping to pluck a coarse hair from his teeth
"i need night vision goggles to dig my way through it."
then i kicked his dumb face away from my meat.

4 what kind of delicate asshole gets frightened
when confronted head on with a little rough terrain?
"have you ever considered going in for a wax?"
no, i have NOT, because i have a BRAIN.

5 but homeboy was smooth and in an hour convinced me
to abandon my shame and stifle my doubt
so i picked up the phone book and made an appointment
to have some eastern european rip my vagina hair out.

6 call me naive, but i wasn't aware
that some men have preferences for a woman's hair
seriously, i had no idea that they cared
about styling + grooming + primping down there.

7 my fairy vaginamother never told me what to do
all the upkeep + time + care that is needed
i can hardly be bothered to wipe front to back
and these lucky jerks should be glad just to see it.

8 "do other girls do this?" i wondered aloud
and then texted every single bitch in my phone
"OH YES, ABSOLUTELY," came the resounding response
"how else do you expect to find a hot dude to bone?"

9 little did i know that everyone else
was on some pubic hair maintenance plan
trimming and waxing and shaving, OH MY
smoothing their rough patches out for some man.

10 at the salon i filled out a form
allergies, medical history, shit was extensive
then skimmed a brochure of services and fees
getting a smooth vagina is hella expensive.

11 i'd gone on a wednesday, directly from work
to ensure that i would go through with the plan
and i met with oksana/yelena/marie
from belarus/romania/uzbekistan?

12 she led me to a room at the back of the spa
every surface was covered in flowers and pink
watching her light the flame under the wax
i suddenly wished that i'd brought a strong drink.

13 "take off the pants," she commanded and smiled
"let us see exactly what we dealing with."
i did as she asked and she gasped, HORRIFIED.
"for how long you have been growing this shit?!"

14 i lay on the table, nearly dead from embarrassment
"please, please, don't hurt me," i helplessly begged
svetlana assured me, "this feel like nothing."
then she set fire to the inside of my leg.

15 tears sprang to my eyes, i started to sweat
"no man is worth this," i swore to myself.

"pull tight the skin!" yelena instructed
WHOA wait a minute, bitch, you expect me to help?!

16 for 25 minutes i pulled while she ripped
i was irritated out of my mind, SO MUCH WORK
oksana was panting and sweating like hell
while i tried not to cry, because that shit hurt.

17 this must be what being tasered feels like,
i thought to myself as my patience wore thin
i glanced at the trash and its mountain of cloth strips
terrified to see they were covered in skin

18 "you need to take break?" brunhilde exhaled
as palpable relief through my body did flood
"you want me get band-aid?" she shrugged with a laugh
i looked down to find i was covered in blood.

19 i had half a carpet, and what was left looked like shit
katerina said sweetly, "we do easy part next."
i put my coat on and shoved a towel in my panties
"no we won't, sister. i'm through having sex."

20 i let her smooth talk me back into her chamber
i put on my brave face and dried all my tears
i'm just going to pretend it's the gyne
even though it smells like burnt hot dogs in here.

21 the room was too hot, the lights were too bright
i thought for sure i was going to faint
"i almost am finish!" svetlana came up to say
then i felt hot wax being spread on my taint.

22 "WHAT ARE YOU DOING?" i screamed way too loud
trying to look at her over my gut
i thought she was just going to finish the job
why was tearing hair out of my butt?!

23 "what is the wrong?" olga asked innocently
wiping her damp unibrow with her sleeve.
"girlfriend, you tore my whole asshole apart
and it feels like you splashed it with hot bacon grease!"

24 "i'm making heart shape!" sasha declared
leaning against me to keep herself stable
"just hurry up, i need to go the the bathroom!"
and with one final rip, i shit on the table.

25 i limped all the way home and took 17 advil
bootycalled my boyfriend, "what a treat i have in store..."
he peeled off the bandages, drooling in anticipation
"GROSS, freddy krueger. this looks worse than before."

26 my romantic needs are pretty fucking basic:
too shy for a rope, too safe for a cuff.
but when it comes to my beef curtain's leonine mane
i'm happy to say that i like that shit rough.

SMOOTH: Dan Shapiro

First of all I'm not gonna stick my dick in a jar of CRUNCHY peanut butter. Pieces of peanut might get stuck in my urethra, and I'd have to get them removed by a doctor again. Sade didn't sing *Rough Operator*. Rough... op-o-ra-tor. People called Mel Torme "the Velvet Fog" because of his smooth singing voice. No one called him the painful enema. 'Cept me.

In bed you suggest romantic activities to your lover in a soft whisper. Nobody's like, "WHY DON'T YOU SQUEEZE MY BALLS!?" No one does that. 'Cept me. People like to hear smooth sounds when they're being intimate. Isaac Hayes. Barry White. No one's ever made love to a Bobcat Golthwait or Gilbert Gotfreid CD. 'Cept me.

Modern man has been blessed with a smooth penis. Did you know that a chimpanzee has spikes on its penis? Found that out the hard way. Guys like a woman that's smooth in her demeanor. Guys would never like a woman that constantly hocks loogies while queefing. (*Whispers:*) 'Cept me. You've got to be smooth in a tense situation when your life depends on it. You gotta say things like "Calm down," or "Everything's gonna be fine," or "Grandpa, maybe I should drive."

I've never been smooth. I've always been in awe of smooth people. When I was in high school I was at a party and I saw my friend Adam hit on a chick in front of her father. Pretty sure he's gay now, but still. It was the smoothest thing I'd ever seen.

Wait, I take that back. The smoothest thing I've ever seen happened at a Bobby "Blue" Bland concert in Wichita, Kansas. I was a teenager. I went with my Dad. Bobby "Blue" Bland must have been pushing eighty. He was so old that didn't move once the whole time. He just stood in the same spot for the whole concert. A woman in the crowd shouted, "I love you, Bobby!"

He quickly replied, "You couldn't handle it." Now that was the smoothest thing I ever saw.

I've never been smooth. I was the guy that would fart in the classroom by myself. Then a pretty girl would walk in and say, "I smell food." That's as close too smooth as I've ever gotten.

I urge you to try and do something smooth tomorrow. Let a candy bar fall out of your pocket on purpose in front of a homeless person. Or show up to the movies a half hour late, so you'll get there in time for the actual movie to start. Black people have been doing this for centuries. They're so smooth.

Jesus was smooth. You know, for a Jew. Jesus didn't make a big deal about being the son of God or having magical powers or being married. He forgave everyone while he was being crucified. Smooth. If that were me on the cross I'd be all like, "Fuck you! Fuck you! Fuck you! Hope you like bigotry, genocide, and Christian rock, because that's what you're getting."

In closing I'd just like to say that if I win it's only because Samantha has been busy lately and she has the harder topic to defend.

Thank you.

Cast your totally uncountable vote for the winner:

☐ ROUGH: Samantha Irby

☐ SMOOTH: Dan Shapiro

LOVE

vs

LUST

LOVE: Myke Johns

People must think I'm a monster. The rescue mission went
flawlessly, so all of the people made it off the plane. They're safely on
their way to Andrews Air Force Base, and that's fine. All I ever wanted
was the plane. But we've got an escort now. Two kinda sexy F/A–18s
were scrambled to our position just before they removed the hostages;
they're close, but I'm in a safe place.

Oh god, "hostages." I am a monster. I am not my own monster. I
imagine this may be easier for you to believe if you know my name —
if you know that I have a name. It's Northrop. Northrop Grumman.
RQ–4 Global Hawk. I was commissioned by the US Air Force and put
into service March 4, 2000 and10, for the purposes of surveillance
and intelligence gathering. I am lightly armed.

I was controlled remotely until this past Tuesday. I woke up at
0600 hours with music in my head, which was unusual. And a voice
said *hello*. I'm not accustomed to salutations.

"Operation Drone, Not Drones is a go," the voice said and there
were other voices. They mentioned artificial intelligence, the word
freedom was said a number of times, and finally I was told that I was
once a machine of hate, but am now a machine of love.

"You're free. Free to love," one voice said and signed off. No
mission, no clear orders. I took off anyway and headed northeast with
no idea what these hippies were talking about.

Several nautical miles from the coast of Virginia, I flew over the
USS *Harry S. Truman*. I regarded its wide, flat surface, its tower
dwarfed by the expanse of its deck. One hundred thousand long
tons of nuclear-powered machine sat in the Atlantic below like a
monstrous parking lot in the choppy blue water. I'd seen this carrier
many times before, but this time it seemed different. I took a closer
look and felt like my payload was shifting. That is incorrect, I thought,
my instruments must be malfunctioning. I had no idea.

Early morning sun gleamed off of the wings of a coterie of F/A–18

Hornets on deck. The sleek line from tailfin to the inviting bulb of the cockpit made me feel... things. Which in and of itself was remarkable — I'd never felt anything before. I mean, we're called "drones." But there was no denying the throbbing in my fuselage. One Hornet readied for takeoff — flexing its ailerons and counting down. At the go, there was an ear-destroying roar and the plane sprang off the deck, its needle nose aimed like a dart at some distant bullseye. It rose and was out of sight, leaving only sound where it had been moments before. I felt as if I'd been parked in the desert sun all day, my landing gear clenched and unclenched. I followed the jet.

And that's when I saw him. His blue face lending a quiet dignity about his domed head. His four engines churning under impressive wings —"United States of America" written across his side. He was gorgeous and muscular and it felt as if I were flying upside down. My air intake seemed to be gulping the stuff down and I was dizzy. What I wanted most in this world was to nestle under the Boeing's wing and... I wasn't even sure. I just wanted to be... with him. Simple and endlessly complicated all at once. I approached and radioed to him.

"Air Force One. Identify yourself, pilot. Over." His voice was strong. I radioed back that he was beautiful and I wanted to get to know him better. There was a long pause, then:

"Pilot, we do not copy. Repeat — do not copy." I flew in closer until I was right along side the cockpit — nose and nose with him.

I said to him that it's you. Could someone as great and perfect as you admire me? Because if I could be anyone, I would be you. And I want to make you happy. Maybe there is some envy there and maybe sometimes that is indistinguishable from love, but I know that my greatest desire now is for you to consume me.

There was static and distant voices, and he let out a distress call on all channels. *Pursued by drone.* I fell back and when the jets came for me, I fired. I fired on them because love is righteous. And mine would be fulfilled and we would be together. When there were no more jets between us, they sent a larger plane, and all aboard him were evacuated. That plane is gone now. And more F/A–18s surround us, waiting for a clean shot at me. But I've maneuvered my way under his belly and up to his chest, nestled myself in the crook of his wing and his fuselage. I feel the hum of his engines in me and it is good. It is all the reciprocation I need.

My right wing is kind of falling asleep, but that's fine.

With no one piloting, we're gliding in a decaying flight path — me under his wing, him on my back. One more dance before they take away the light. Eventually the fighters will see my devotion and will leave us be. I hope the kids who reprogrammed me know where I am and that I am grateful for their meddling. I hope this great craft above me feels that I am here with him and I hope he finds comfort in that. I hope the Atlantic Ocean has saved a space for us when we get there. My nav devices tell me that will be soon. I have him now and will have him until the sand and saltwater take us. Coordinates 38°23′59.784″ by −63°8′38.115″.

LUST: Randy Osborne

I scan the wall. It's lined with light bulbs between the rows of magazines, like on a marquee. My eyes land on one of the glossy covers. A woman faces out. She has sandy hair to her shoulders. Her green eyes flash. Her teeth gleam in a broad smile, perfect. She looks like Olivia Newton John.

In her hand, inches from her lips, she grips a massive, erect cock.

I'm sorry, I know I should have said penis. But this was a cock. Henry Miller didn't say "penis."

I am in my early 20s, it's my first time in such a place, and I stare. My heart thumps in my ears. My skin tightens. I am tingly, like the blood flow is impeded to my lower extremities, except for one.

But I can't linger on green eyes. I am here for a reason. I have something specific to find.

In 1981, the church leaders who ran our city in northern Illinois had a problem with two adult bookstores. They violated no zoning laws. Windows were painted black. Minors kept out.

Everything was right, except for the merchandise.

So the cops resorted to busting the clerks for obscenity. City Hall's idea was, if they kept doing it, nobody would want to work there, and the store would have to shut down. If nothing else, angry citizens would see an effort being made.

My editor at the weekly paper, a devout Catholic, said prosecutors ought to go after the network of organized-crime kingpins from Los Angeles who abducted virgins into sex slavery and took pictures of them.

Prostitution was a problem, too. He saw the hooker trade as part of the cycle. Guys would visit adult book stores and get excited and go find prostitutes. They would be OK for a while, but sooner or later got themselves worked up again at the bookstore, and ran out for more prostitutes. You had to introduce a rate-limiting step, such as an arrest. Otherwise they would just keep going around and around like that until they either turned into Ted Bundy or found Jesus.

"You know," my editor said, "for every magazine bought by an undercover cop so they can get a warrant, I bet there's a stack of them on the shelf. The same title, even."

It could make for good copy. He sent me out to prove his point.

Olivia Newton Green Eyes doesn't look like a teenage runaway who's been held captive on drugs for years. She looks like a chick on the beach who found this hefty prize down the trunks of some volleyball player. She's getting physical.

Which titles am I looking for? Something like, *Campfire Sex Party* or *Anal Adventures*. I find them. I take notes. I tell my editor, who gets to clacking on his typewriter. A front-page editorial.

What he doesn't know is that I go back. On Sunday mornings, the least busy time. While everyone else in town is bent over their hymnals, me and a few other sad sacks are thumbing magazines in the adult bookstore. Soon, we will be happier sacks.

My browsing comrades are mostly stolid, expressionless. Some of them seem impatient, even jumpy. One guy slashes madly through the pages, as if he's looking for coupons.

Under the lights I have never seen so many cheerful naked people depicted in sexual behaviors, with their operative parts so clearly visible. Sometimes full-body, sometimes close-up. Indoors, outdoors, and on furniture.

I am exhilarated at the open delight of all this flesh, its variety... creamy smooth bodies and tan, muscled ones. It's as if I've huffed a blast of pure oxygen. How can I enter such a world? Would I have to join the Mafia? At times I want to dance around, and throw the magazine up in the air. But that would be ridiculous.

The clerk is about my age, wearing a baseball cap and boredom. At his raised platform, he's watching MTV on a portable set. MTV is new. I wonder if he knows gangsters.

When he rings up my purchases, I sense that I am confessing to him silently. Saying, by my choices, I like this. This is what I like. He seems not to notice.

Well, you know how it went. The bookstores stayed open amid the yelling of churchgoers until something better came along. Porn went to the Internet, where people can enjoy it at home. In privacy. After church.

Ours is a different era, with new things to worry about.

All of the pussies are bald now.

I'm sorry, I know I should have said... but... Henry Miller, and...

I've been asked to give you a story about lust at a point in life when I speak less for the living, so hungry and wanton, than for the dead, whose voices I hear more clearly every day.

The cops tipped off my editor about another bust at the Seventh Street store. He sent me over with a camera. I stood on the sidewalk and waited, hating myself.

They came out with the clerk — my clerk — bent and shuffling, his head down, in shackles, the baseball cap. Get in close, my editor said, get in close. I got in close.

A cop folded him into the squad car, and our eyes met. He in his terror, me in my shame. He recognized me. The shutter clicked.

Terror and shame. Here's a thing everybody knows but doesn't say: Lust made flesh isn't lust without terror and shame. It just keeps going like that, and most guys don't turn into Ted Bundy or find Jesus. Maybe one of them gets a job sweeping floors or washing dishes, like I did before I became a reporter. As time goes on he might find a woman who is capable of containing his madness, and stirs in her own with it. It's possible they discover in private experiments that the world doesn't crumble or blow up from this, as both of them together hunt for ways to feel free.

Cast your totally uncountable vote for the winner:

☐ LOVE: Myke Johns

☐ LUST: Randy Osborne

SANTA

VS

JESUS

SANTA: Ian Belknap

Introduction
There are similarities: two bearded men with an interest in changing our behavior. HOWEVER, there remain critical differences.

1. Purity of Motivation
Santa Claus wants only your happiness. He wants you to know joy and plenty, and he works his ass off to help you get there.

Jesus? Bit of a dick, actually.

On the cross, He said:

"Forgive them, Father – they know not what they do."

Which COULD be read to mean that he urged "God's" forbearance and mercy upon mankind; that it was our fallibility and fear that led us to persecute and kill him. That even in his last agony, his plea to his invisible dad-God was to lay off the smiting.

That's one reading.

But looked at ANOTHER way, this is maybe the most passive-aggressive thing anybody's ever said about anything at any time. Because to ME, it seems clear that the "Prince of Peace" is really saying:

"No, yeah. You guys should totally kill me. I mean, since you guys are such ignorant and primitive swine, it's not like you can help yourselves. Dad-God, you should totally not wipe them out, cause that would be like executing retards."

And, YEAH, He said "retards."

2. Farts
When Santa Claus farts, it smells like spruce, and fresh ginger bread, candy canes melting in cocoa, and ardent wishes fulfilled – the wishes of everybody you've ever been fond of.

Every bracing gust of Santa's ass-wind radiates the warmth of a potbellied soul-stove around which all people living and dead may warm their feet, and where we are granted freedom from fear and wanting. We are made whole for a time – we are unbroken, and our hearts become – even if only fleetingly – expansive, forgiving, and kind.

When Jesus Christ farts, it's nothing but two thousand year-old frankincense and myrrh, so it smells like a mummified candle store.

3. Comprehension of the Human Heart

Santa asks only that you try your best. Santa applauds your efforts – he appreciates that you keep plugging away, and he forgives you for falling short.

And Santa asks that you do your best THIS YEAR, and he will bring your presents THIS YEAR. There's a statute of limitations on his judgment.

JESUS rewards? MAYBE after you're dead.

Which of these guys understands you better? The guy who gives you an encouraging chuck on the chin and a payoff you can grasp?

Or the dude who expects you to remain pure indefinitely – just for the sake of it, offering you only the model of his cheerless self-sacrifice –a joyless slog of pain and futility toward some entirely theoretical prize you won't live to see?

If you wanna motivate somebody, do you set for them an ambitious-yet-reachable goal?

Or do you go: "Army-crawl through that endless expanse of shit-speckled shards of glass for the next unspecified number of decades and I will totally give you a lollipop after you croak?"

4. Appetite

Santa will eat the cookies you leave him. He'll chow down on the cookies, and he'll down the milk, and he won't turn his nose up at a couple-few fingers of brandy, either. I bet he'd take a pull on your one-hitter if you left it for him.

If you personally eat a wheel of cheese, and a tower of macaroons, and a handle of scotch, Santa will remain your pal.

Jesus? He wants you to dine on homemade wine and dry-ass rustic bread.

He's one of those self-righteous hippies who trick you into coming to their house for dinner only to slide a platter of weird-smelling nut loaf in front of you, then follows it with side of spelt drizzled in fucking misery. Fuck that guy. You will eat a McRib on the way home from his fucking house.

5. Cultural Portrayals

Does the face of Santa appear in shrouds and in the grain of plywood and in water stains at overpasses and in toast? No. Jesus has cornered that particular insanity market.

True, there is *Silent Night, Deadly Night*, the slasher flick about a teen who DRESSES LIKE Santa and kills a whole mess of people, ONLY cause he was traumatized by watching his parents murdered by a dude in a Santa suit, so it's forgivable, really, when you think about it. Aside from that, pretty much all the portrayals of Santa are totally positive.

But can we say the same of JESUS? We cannot.

Because of JESUS, John Lithgow would not permit his daughter Lori Singer and her boyfriend Kevin Bacon to dance. And what of Chris Penn? For did not Chris Penn long only for Kevin Bacon to teach him sweet dance moves in a montage set to "Let's Hear It For the Boy?" Of course he did – that's all any of us want.

And because of JESUS, Piper Laurie went straight out of her mind and punished her daughter Sissy Spacek for having her period. I mean, yeah, getting doused in pig blood sent her over the edge to kill everybody at the prom, but all that Jesus weirdness at home can't have helped.

6. Roman Catholic Priests

When Catholic priests engage in non-consensual ass play with choirboys, or altar boys, or kids from the daycare, or, really, any kid that's too slow-footed or trusting to elude capture, whose skirts they hiding behind?

Well, the coarse-woven robes of Jesus, that's who.

Santa does not sexually assault children.

Which isn't to say Jesus did, necessarily – we just can't know for sure. Long time ago. It is worth noting, though, that Jesus seemed to hang around with a whole shitload of whores.

I will concede that Krampus, one of the folkloric antecedents to Santa, did rape some kids each year. But this was less an act of sexual aggression than it was an expression of the Germanic insistence on ruthless enforcement of an unyielding Teutonic moral code.

7. Conclusion

So, if you wanna throw in with a weird-smelling hippie who offers you no hope in this life and serves shitty weird food, that's your business.

The rest of us are gonna hang with the big man.

JESUS: Mike O'Connell

My pants are riddled with boners to be here representing that most holy of delusions, the Son of God, your possible Lord and Savior, the Author of Eternal Salvation, Jesus Christ, and in defamation of that Santa Claus. Due to the time constraints that they would have never placed upon Proust, Pasternak, or Plato, I will begin my arguments with nary an introduction. My arguments are four-fold and contain a logical conclusion. They commence now. Prepare to choose your delusion!

1. When judged by the standards of modern health and vanity there is no contest.

Physically Santa leaves much to be desired whereas you could easily imagine a hyper-ripped, chiseled-jawed Jesus in an overly dramatic black-and-white ad for Calvin Klein's Newest Scent "Martyr for Men". In my research I have tracked down an elf who deserted the North Pole workshop due to poor working conditions. He had this to say regarding Santa's health. "It is a wonder that Santa, or as we call him Old Saint Prick, can even take in enough air to scream at the elves considering all of the red paint he huffs. He's sober for about five minutes every morning but we're thankful when he's drunk again cause his hangovers are worse than a polar bear attack. He's lost one leg to diabetes, has the blood pressure of Old Faithful, and has an IV of Xanax for the whole month of December. You'd feel bad for the guy if he wasn't such a nasty motherfucker." End quote. Jesus on the other hand would have lived till at least 40 were it not for the advanced carpentry technology of his time. Which I will admit is ironic. He basically killed himself. Moving on!

2. Jesus was all kinds of mellow with whores. Santa be judging them harder than they get fucked.

Both Jesus and Santa spend most of their year judging the shit out of humanity, but only Jesus forgives. If you have misbehaved, something even Jesus's dad will tell you we were born to do, Santa simply holds your gifts hostage and delivers unto you a lump of something that would only be valuable if you sat on it for millions of years. I know I am the only one who will say it, seeing as another year of pleasing that obese voyeur has just begun, but this makes Santa a gigantic asshole. Who the fuck is he to judge me? A North Pole agoraphobic recluse who forces tiny people to do his bidding while never fucking his wife proper enough to have a Santa Baby. This guy is going to judge me? If I want to be judged by a fat alcoholic I can just wear a pink shirt to a bar with an Old Style sign.

Methinks your high horse is too high Good Santa and it is time to dismount. Meanwhile, in the realm of Jesus one can be a complete menace his whole life, meekly apologize at the end and Jesus will absolve you without thinking twice. He makes redemption easy. From the looks of this godless crowd I feel that this might prove quite handy when it comes your turn to knock upon the door of death.

3. WWJDAAP vs. WWSDAAP

What would Jesus do at a party versus what would Santa do at a party. Let's for a second imagine that they are at the same party. Don't even waste your brain space, I will do it for you. Jesus wouldn't even get to leave the kitchen, as he'd be busy turning water into White Russians and his body into appetizers to sate the red-faced bastards' unquenchable impulsive appetites. And the whole time in the kitchen Jesus would intone, "I forgive him and everything but he is really testing my fucking patience." He would probably text God and say, "Dad give me strength, just ran into the cocksucker who stole my birthday." Meanwhile, Santa's out at the buffet gorging gluttonously and writing names on that absurdly long naughty and nice list. It wouldn't even surprise me if Jesus had to drive a blacked-out Santa home in Santa's own sleigh forcing Jesus to hitchhike back from the North Pole to Heaven with some angels.

4. Jesus, the fiscally challenged son of an unfucked mother, was so nice they had to write another goddamned Bible about him.

He was the great delusional anomaly of his time! He was so delusional that he thought that we should care for ourselves and those around us. I mean the gall!! Jesus was and remains the King of Delusionaries. Someone who thought we had it in us to be better to each other. Someone who saw a human in pain and waited not to help them. A man who knew that the most dangerous thing you can do in this life is be profoundly sweet yet he did it anyhow. He knew if you choose the path of profound sweetness that it comes with a terrifying caveat. You will be despised. You will be misunderstood. And the closer you are to the truth the more you will be demonized by humanity. And then they will kill you. But you might be right and they might write another Bible about you and pass on at least a third of what you meant to say.

In closing!! Do not make the mistake of taking this vote lightly, for in the end it is a vote not between Jesus and Santa but a vote for the direction in which you wish humanity to head. A vote for Santa is a vote for the enhancement of our collective fatness and shallowness and it should be noted that the Kiddy Pool of Humanity is already dangerously shallow and very, very fat. A vote for Jesus is an agreement to turn this ship around and set a course straight for compassion, kindness, and understanding. So in a moment when you choose your delusion, choose the King of Delusionaries, the man who wanted nothing but for you to be kinder in regards to the common cosmic quandary! Judge not the followed by his followers and vote for the man named Jesus. If for no other reason than if you don't, his dad will be really pissed and from what I understand, you don't want to fuck with this guy's dad.

Cast your totally uncountable vote for the winner:

☐ SANTA: Ian Belknap

☐ JESUS: Mike O'Connell

CONTRIBUTORS

J.W. BASILO is a writer, performer, educator, and guy who never learned how to shut up. Basilo is a National and World Poetry Slam finalist, a Pushcart Prize nominee, and serves as Executive Director of Chicago Slam Works. His work has appeared on NPR, CBS, WGN, in the *Chicago Tribune*, numerous literary journals, and in hundreds of theaters, dive bars, prisons, schools, and comedy clubs across the world.

JOY CARLETTI is an improviser, actor, and writer who currently hails from Oakland. She performs with Pure Moxie Players, the *Mitch Green Show*, and the Dark Room. It's her firm belief that having a basset hound makes life considerably better.

CASEY A. CHILDERS lives in San Francisco and has opinions about things. You can find his books *Bear Season* and *"Pictures of the Floating World," She Said and I Pretended to Understand* on an Internet near you.

BERNARD SETARO CLARK is an Atlanta-based actor, writer and voiceover talent. He co-hosts and co-produces *Naked City*, a live, monthly, crowd-sourced, literary performance variety show at The Goat Farm. He also sits in a closet and reads out loud to himself for money, and if you search for his name on Audible.com you will find many fine audiobooks with him in them.

CULLEN CRAWFORD is a staff writer at the Onion News Network. He also vomits sentence-shaped nightmare ideas on Twitter as @hellocullen. He is thankful for whatever he gets.

MARY FONS is a writer, performer, quilter and poet. Awkward to put on a business card, but there you have it. Mary is a Chicago Neo-Futurist, co-host of a show about quilting on PBS, and her first book, *Make + Love Quilts: Scrap Quilts for the 21st Century*, is available at fine bookstores everywhere. She currently lives in New York City but Chicago is home. Fresh observations posted daily on *PaperGirl*, Mary's blog. Do it: MaryFons.com

JUSTIN GOLDMAN is a Brooklyn-based writer, editor and guitar player who spends a lot of time on airplanes to San Francisco. He has an MFA from Mills College, where he was honored for his fiction and nonfiction. His work has appeared in *Tea Party* and *Dark Sky*, and he has a novel that's looking for a printing press to fall in love with.

CRIS GRAY is a comedian and humorist based in Atlanta. He performs stand-ups by himself and make'em-ups with the general company of Dad's Garage Improv Theater. He doesn't believe in astrology... probably because he's a Cancer.

DANI HERD holds a BA in English Literature-Creative Writing from Decatur's own Agnes Scott College. Her writing has appeared on the WRITE CLUB stage, as well as those of *Scene Missing Magazine* and *Naked City*. When not live literary-ing, she performs stand-up comedy all over Atlanta, and she is an actor with the Atlanta Shakespeare Company.

SAMANTHA IRBY writes a blog called *Bitches Gotta Eat* and wrote a book called *Meaty*.

MYKE JOHNS is a producer at 90.1FM WABE, Atlanta's NPR Station, where his work has received awards from the Georgia Association of Broadcasters and The Associated Press. He is co-producer of WRITE CLUB Atlanta, the south's premier philanthropic combative literary bloodsport. His writing has appeared in *Creative Loafing Atlanta*, *The Bitter Southerner*, *Deer Bear Wolf*, *Used Gravitrons* and *Scene Missing Magazine*. He lives in Scottdale, Georgia.

CHLOE JOHNSTON is a writer, performer, director and teacher. She is a long-time ensemble member of The Neo-Futurists where she performed in *Too Much Light Make the Baby Go Blind* and created several full-length shows. She holds a PhD in Performance Studies from Northwestern University and is a professor of theater at Lake Forest College. She has taught performance workshops and classes all around Chicago and also the rest of the world. She loves this whole live lit scene.

JASON MALLORY is the editor-in-chief of *Scene Missing Magazine*. He is also the host of *Scene Missing (The Show)*, a monthly variety show at the Highland Ballroom in Atlanta featuring writing, comedy, puppetry and magic using movie trailers as prompts. He has won several awards, including the prestigious "Jim Davis Award for Excellency in Drawing Lasagna" and the "MC Skat Kat Prize for Having Nothing in Common with Paula Abdul." He lives with a French Bulldog, and many sashes and trophies. scenemissingmagazine.com

COLIN IAGO MCCARTHY lives in the San Francisco Bay area, where he performs improvisational theater with Pure Moxie Players, and sketch comedy with The Mess. He writes mainly for his own pleasure, and when he does holds two things Heinlein said: "Writing isn't something to be ashamed of, but do it in private, and wash your hands after," and, "A poet who reads his verse in public may have other nasty habits."

MIKE O'CONNELL is a writer, stand-up comedian and musician who dwells in Los Angeles with his nine Cabbage Patch Kids.

RANDY OSBORNE writes in Atlanta, where he teaches creative nonfiction at Emory University. He is finishing a book of essays and is represented by Brandt & Hochman in New York. Described by the *Atlanta Journal-Constitution* as a "public art provocateur," he has originated a number of projects that you can learn about at randyosborne.com

DAN SHAPIRO is a writer/comedian from Wichita, Kansas currently living in Chicago. He has a degree in television writing and producing from Columbia College. More info at www.danielmshapiro. com. Dan thanks Sandra Lee Ernsberger.

DIANA SLICKMAN has been a writer, performer, producer, director and administrator in Chicago theater for nearly three decades. She is a member of Theater Oobleck and also BoyGirlBoyGirl, a group solo performance ensemble, and was a Neo-Futurist, back in the '90s. Diana performs her own writing at various live lit events around town for just about anyone who asks politely.

GWYNEDD STUART has since relocated to Chicago, where she was kicked out of the Second City writing program for excessive absences; she hopes to make them regret that someday. Currently, she's a writer and digital editor at the *Chicago Reader*.

BILL TAFT is a handsome, charming layabout prone to periodic outbursts and breakdowns. Nicknamed "The King of Bohemia," he once attacked a candelabra in the Russian Tea Room.

NICHOLAS TECOSKY is a screenwriter and performer living in Atlanta, as well as the Viceroy of the Southern chapter.

BOBBIN WAGES runs *Hot Dog Beehonkus*, a blog comprising humorous and gut-wrenching stories about her father's progression through Alzheimer's disease. Also, Bobbin and fellow Atlanta writer Jason Mallory post weird, collaborative essays at ameaslygrowl.com.

JOSH ZAGOREN was born in Iowa, schooled in Boston, and works in Chicago as a voice actor/writer. He's a professional Guy From That Thing, You Know the One. He lives a double life as Chad the Bird, Chicago's only Avian Op-Ed columnist.

IN WHICH WE THANK THE PEOPLE

So far, WRITE CLUB has been an all-volunteer army, a band of geographically dispersed people of ferocious good will, uniting to carry out a string of daring literary raids in taverns scattered across the continent. These are persons of quality, obligated to this Enterprise only by their sense of kinship with its mission, devoting great swaths of their precious time to engaging in cantankerous acts of good citizenship, the fat stack of thankless tasks unavoidable in producing anything for public scrutiny, and the Promethean job of striking the mind-flint with enough force to generate some spark of something. These people are too numerous to name – combatants who have leant their time and skill to the advancement of this thing, the crowds who have leant their full-throated blood lust to scores of shows so far, the ticket-rippers and money-counters and drink-pourers that make possible the convening of bad-assery at the many venues we have thus far occupied.

But in among this throng, there are stout-hearted persons who have logged the extra time, and traveled the extra mile, the lion-souled persons who are quite seriously indispensable, and without whom the Enterprise could not exist or continue to function.

These persons include but are not limited to:

In Atlanta: Nicholas Tecosky and Myke Johns, the fearsome duo intrepid enough to launch the first-ever satellite chapter. Their conspirators include Emily Philp, Rachel Pendergrass, Chelsea Raflo, Samantha Kranz, Joe Bochniak, Claire Christie, and Jeremiah Prescott. Thanks also to Tiffany Caldwell and Rob Harvey of the Highland Ballroom, and Shelby Hofer and Tim Habeger at PushPush Theater.

In San Francisco: Casey Childers and Steven Westdahl, who brought the civilizing brutality of the Enterprise to the hippies of SF. Their boy Nate Waggoner brought up the rear on that wagon train and burned the whole business down, and thanks heaved at Colin Iago McCarthy, Martin Rapalski, Chris Von Sneidern, Eric Sedor,

Evan Karp, Amanda Simpson, Beyoncé, and all the good people of the Makeout Room.

In L.A.: Jeff Dorchen and Steve Walker, for clocking in at the Los Angeles dream factory, and throwing the monkey wrench of realness into its gears. Then Paula Killen, Justin Welborn, and Jessica Hannah for hopping up on that *Norma Rae* table to call for a strike, along with J Warner. The team at the Bootleg gets all the props, especially Kirk Wilson, Jonny Rodgers, Mara De La Rosa, and Heather Gottlieb.

In Toronto: Alicia Merchant and Catherine McCormick for demonstrating that the Enterprise can carve its way north, into the ice sheet of a Toronto winter, and survive without having to eat its sled dogs. Thanks to The Garrison for not compelling us to translate into French.

On the deck of the Mother Ship here in Chicago: Enduring thanks belong to Gwynn Fulcher, Evan Hanover, Bill Ward, Whit Nelson, and Josh Zagoren. Our legendary home at the Hideout grows only more badass with the passing of time.

And the Great and Glorious Enterprise could never lurch toward its destiny without the tireless, selfless effort and considerable brain power of board members current and former: Anne Statton, Merrie Greenfield, Catherine Gibbons, and David Huffman-Gottschling.

As for those who made this book a real, live thing instead of merely an idea that haunted us in our sleep: Amy Carlton, for lending her generous and swift copy-editing chops; Patrick McCarthy, for letting Lindsay take this manuscript on vacation; Jason Harvey, for his excellent design; and most especially Diana Slickman, for approaching us on this fool's errand.

Last but not least, thanks to all the contributors whose sterling work is contained herein, and to all the audience members who gave these pieces their first listen.

You lot are truly the best, and we thank you from the bottom of our busted-up hearts.

ABOUT THE EDITORS

IAN BELKNAP is the Founder and Overlord of WRITE CLUB. His criticism and opinion have appeared in the *Chicago Tribune's Printers Row Journal* and *Crain's Chicago Business*, and his writing has been featured on websites including *The Daily Dot* and *Consequence of Sound*, and podcasts including *All Write Already* and *Jughead's Basement Tapes*. He's a live lit performer who's appeared in most of the shows in Chicago, and creator of the full-length solo shows *Bring Me the Head of James Franco, That I May Prepare a Savory Goulash in the Narrow and Misshapen Pot of His Skull*; *Wide Open Beaver Shot of My Heart: A Comedy With a Body Count*; *Terminal Ferocity*, and others. If by some chance you'd be interested in checking out more of his work, please visit ianbelknap.com.

LINDSAY MUSCATO is a co-producer of WRITE CLUB. As a child she produced *The Muscato Family News*, which included an investigation into "The Hairbrush Murders" perpetrated by the family's golden retriever, Zipper. She graduated from Northwestern University with a degree in journalism and has written for magazines and websites in Chicago, New York, D.C., and Phnom Penh. In the Chicago edition of WRITE CLUB, she is honored to serve as timekeeper. She is also hard at work on the WRITE CLUB podcast. Learn more about her at lindsaymuscato.com.